Future education: learning the future
Scenarios and strategies in Europe

Fons van Wieringen
Burkart Sellin
Ghislaine Schmidt

Cedefop Reference series; 42
Luxembourg: Office for Official Publications of the European Communities, 2003

A great deal of additional information on the European Union is available on the Internet.
It can be accessed through the Europa server (http://europa.eu.int).

Cataloguing data can be found at the end of this publication.

Luxembourg: Office for Official Publications of the European Communities, 2003

ISBN 92-896-0200-7
ISSN 1608-7089

© European Centre for the Development of Vocational Training, 2003
All rights reserved.

Printed in Belgium

PRINTED ON WHITE CHLORINE-FREE PAPER

The **European Centre for the Development of Vocational Training** (Cedefop) is the European Union's reference centre for vocational education and training. We provide information on and analyses of vocational education and training systems, policies, research and practice.
Cedefop was established in 1975 by Council Regulation (EEC) No 337/75.

Europe 123
GR-57001 Thessaloniki (Pylea)

Postal address: PO Box 22427
GR-55102 Thessaloniki

Tel. (30) 23 10 49 01 11, Fax (30) 23 10 49 00 20
E-mail: info@cedefop.eu.int
Homepage: www.cedefop.eu.int
Interactive website: www.trainingvillage.gr

Fons van Wieringen,
Burkart Sellin,
Ghislaine Schmidt

Edited by:
Cedefop
Burkart Sellin, *Project Manager*

Published under the responsibility of:
Johan van Rens, *Director*
Stavros Stavrou, *Deputy Director*

Table of contents

Preface 5
Executive summary 7

1. **Scenarios and strategies** 19
1.1. Strategic planning in VET and LLL 19
1.2. Strategies and actors in VET systems 23
1.3. Scenario construction 25

2. **Design of the project** 33
2.1. Design of phase 1 33
2.2. Design of phase 2 43

3. **Constructing the scenarios** 51
3.1. A six step procedure to arrive at the scenarios 51
3.2. Provisional scenarios at European level as discussed in phase 1 52
3.3. Provisional scenarios at national levels 60
3.4. Contours of overarching scenarios at European level 62
3.5. Improved scenarios at national levels (2nd phase) 65
3.6. Clusters of scenarios at European level 72
3.7. Questionnaire on EU-level 83
3.8. Links with recent EU scenario developments 84

4. **Development of strategies** 87
4.1. Strategy development in phase 1 87
4.2. Further development of strategies (phase 2) 90
4.3. Comparing recent EU policy strategies with the strategies developed in this project 104

5. **Robustness of strategies vis-à-vis scenarios** 109
5.1. (Rules regarding) demand articulation 110
5.2. (Rules regarding) supply variety 111
5.3. (Rules regarding) information availability 112
5.4. Coordination 113

6. Relevant EU-level actors on strategy and scenario interaction   117
6.1. Strategies   118
6.2. Scenarios   123
6.3. Robustness   127
6.4. Concluding remarks   131

7. The scenario method   135
7.1. The method as used in this project   135
7.2. Experiences with the method   136
    7.2.1. Education and human resource development   136
    7.2.2. Getting the data   137
    7.2.3. Beyond the short term   139
    7.2.4. European impact   140
    7.2.5. Actors and implementation   141
7.3. Improvement of the method   142
7.4. Conditions for application   148
    7.4.1. Open planning   148
    7.4.2. Learning instrument for policy makers   149
    7.4.3. Adapting the methodology   151
7.5. European level experience   152
7.6. Strengths and weaknesses   153
    7.6.1. Strengths   153
    7.6.2. Weaknesses   154

8. Annex I   157
8.1. Overview of 'national' scenarios and strategies   157
    8.1.1. Austria   157
        8.1.1.1. Scenario I – Internationalisation   157
        8.1.1.2. Scenario II – Harmonisation   159
        8.1.1.3. Scenario III – Regionalisation   161
    8.1.2. Czech Republic   163
        8.1.2.1. Scenario I – Scepticism to changes   163
        8.1.2.2. Scenario II – Growth – Solidarity   167
        8.1.2.3. Scenario III – Growth – Competitiveness   172
    8.1.3. Estonia   177
        8.1.3.1. Scenario I – Good Start   177
        8.1.3.2. Scenario II – Splitting into Two   179
        8.1.3.3. Scenario III – Dissolving   181

8.1.4. Greece		183
8.1.4.1.	Scenario I – Complete Domination of the Market and Increased Inequalities on Multiple Levels	183
8.1.4.2.	Scenario II – 'Individual and Selective Responses to the Effects of Globalisation'	192
8.1.4.3.	Scenario III – Competitive economy - life long learning - new dimensions in social policy	198
8.1.5. Luxembourg/Belgium		206
8.1.5.1.	Scenario I – Controlled Globalisation	206
8.1.5.2.	Scenario II – State Regulation	210
8.1.5.3.	Scenario III – Proximity of Training	214
8.1.6. Poland		218
8.1.6.1.	Scenario I – Limited Development/ Ad hoc Adjustments	218
8.1.6.2.	Scenario II – Growth, Cooperation and Competition	223
8.1.7. Slovenia		229
8.1.7.1.	Scenario I – Economic and Social Crisis	229
8.1.7.2.	Scenario II – Slow and Steady (controlled) Growth	233
8.1.7.3.	Scenario III – Economic Growth and Flexibility	236
8.1.8. United Kingdom		239
8.1.8.1.	Scenario I – Crisis Looms and the Big Players step in	239
8.1.8.2.	Scenario II – Ad hoc Response to Global Pressure	242
8.1.8.3.	Scenario III – A The free-market approach to competitiveness on course (UK Scenario 1)	244
8.1.8.4.	Scenario III – B A Social Partnership Approach to Competitiveness Develops (UK Scenario 3)	247

9.	**Annex II**	**251**
9.1.	Scenario/strategy methods	251
10.	**Annex III**	**257**
11.	**Annex IV**	**259**
12.	**Annex V**	**263**
12.1.	List of country reports	263
13.	**Annex VI**	**265**
13.1.	References	265
14.	**Selected Cedefop publications**	**269**

Preface

In 1998 the European Centre for the Development of Vocational Training (Cedefop) launched a call for manifestation of interest, asking for partners in a study to develop scenarios and strategies for vocational education and training (VET) in Europe. Following this call institutes from several EU Member States and Central and Eastern European countries (CEEs) showed interest to participate and the European Training Foundation based in Turin was included as a sponsor. The institutes that were finally included are five research institutes covering five European Union Member States (Austria, Germany, Greece, Luxembourg/Belgium, United Kingdom) and five research bodies from CEEs (Czech Republic, Estonia, Hungary, Poland and Slovenia).

The scenario project aims to develop a tool to improve the understanding of vocational education and training systems in their economic-technological, employment-labour and training-knowledge environments. The development of different scenarios and the indication of linked strategies serve as one of the bases for discussing relevant policies for VETin a medium and longer term perspective. The development of scenarios for vocational education and training is not intended to and cannot reveal the future; it is in fact intended only to call attention to some of the factors of strategic importance for the shaping of European VET and LLL during the next ten years.

In 1999, the first phase of the project was successfully implemented. The process and its results are described in the report Scenarios and Strategies for Vocational Education and Training in Europe, European Synthesis report on phase 1, authors B. Sellin, F. van Wieringen, H. Dekker, M. Tessaring & A. Fetsi (2001, MGK.01-50).

The second phase started in April 2000 and is completed through the final European level conference in Tallinn/Estonia in October 2001 at which a pre-final version of this report was presented and discussed for the first time jointly with the basic document prepared by Cedefop and ETF describing and discussing the out-comes of the whole project, phase 1 and 2. After this Tallinn Conference a small scale questionnaire was set up to see whether experts at the EU-level are able to work with the constructed strategies and scenarios combinations elaborated in the framework of a transnational/European analysis of outcomes. The results of this are reported in chapter 6 and in annex 4.

There is no standard methodology for developing scenarios and strategies. This made the project all the more interesting for the participants. Not only the possible substantial outcomes of the project motivated the research team members, also its contribution to the clarification of a methodology for the development of scenarios encouraged all participants to invest more in the project than in a more standardised and routine project. The nine to ten participating countries were highly engaged in this 'development project' which makes use of a mixture of quantitative and qualitative methods and which tries to closely combine scenario development with strategies and their ranking in importance, relevance and robustness. The co-ordinating team of Cedefop/ETF and Max Goote Expert Center at the University of Amsterdam is therefore most grateful to their tutoring bodies which had the courage to start and finance such a project, but even more so to the research partners in the participating countries for their consistent, skilful and creative participation.

Stavros Stavrou, Deputy Director/Cedefop,
Burkart Sellin, Project Coordinators/Cedefop
Ulrich Hillenkamp, Deputy Director/ ETF
Peter Grootings, Project Coordiators/ETF

Executive summary

In 1998 the European Centre for the Development of Vocational Training (Cede-fop) launched a call for manifestation of interest, asking for partners in a study to develop scenarios and strategies for vocational education and training (VET) in Europe. Following this call institutes from several EU Member States and Central and Eastern European countries (CEEs) showed interest to participate and the European Training Foundation based in Turin was included as a sponsor. The institutes that were finally included are five research institutes covering five European Union Member States (Austria, Germany, Greece, Luxembourg/Belgium, United Kingdom) and five research bodies from CEEs (Czech Republic, Estonia, Hungary, Poland and Slovenia).

The scenario project aims to develop a tool to improve the understanding of vocational education and training systems in their economic-technological, employment-labour and training-knowledge environments. The development of different scenarios and the indication of linked strategies serve as one of the bases for discussing relevant policies for VET. The development of scenarios for vocational education and training is not intended to and cannot reveal the future; it is in fact intended only to call attention to some of the factors of strategic importance for the shaping of European VET during the next ten years. Factors that can be used in a strategic conversation about possible futures of European VET systems.

In 1999, the first phase of the project was successfully implemented. The process and its results are described in the report Scenarios and Strategies for Vocational Education and Training in Europe, European Synthesis report on phase 1, authors B. Sellin, F. van Wieringen, H. Dekker, M. Tessaring and A. Fetsi (2001, MGK.01-50).

The second phase started in April 2000 and is completed with a final conference in Tallinn in October 2001 and the publication of this report (April 2002).

Dimensions and descriptors

Vocational education and training is situated in three specific contexts. Three questionnaires were developed, each covering one of the contexts/dimensions. The three dimensions are:
- economic dimension;
- social-labour dimension;
- training dimension.

In the training, skills and knowledge dimension only the demand site of training was to be taken into account. For each dimension several descriptors were distinguished. Each dimension had about 17 descriptors (that could be classified into approximately 9 categories). The scenarios had to be written using these descriptors. It was decided that all countries had to use at least the four main descriptors in each dimension:

Economic dimension:	Restructuring, growth, competition, privatisation;
Social-labour dimension:	Flexibility/mobility, work/training patterns, inequalities, organisation of labour;
Training dimension:	General skills, in company training, willingness to invest, lifelong learning.

To enhance the comparability, the countries were asked to quantify the descriptors, using a 5-point scale. They had to give the 12 descriptors above a score between 1-5, where 1 stood for few/little/weak and 5 for many/much/strong.

Scenarios

The scenarios have been constructed in this project according to a 6-step iterative procedure as follows

(a) The first was the selection of relevant scenario dimensions on the base of the outcomes of all the 10 participating countries in the first phase of the project. This step resulted in two dimensions for each context. Consequently four provisional scenarios were constructed for each context (with the exception of context C for which 2 times four scenarios were developed).

(b) Based on these groups of four scenarios the participating countries developed for their national situation also provisional scenarios for the different contexts.

(c) Based on the scenarios from step 1 and 2 i.e. the scenarios constructed from the European overall database and the scenarios constructed by each national team the main common characteristics were selected and put together in a sketch for common scenarios to be used by the (by then 9) participating countries in order to improve their provisional scenarios.

(d) This step resulted in improved scenarios for each of the 9 participating countries i.e. in total 27 scenarios. These scenarios have their value and meaning in the national context and because they have been constructed vis-à-vis the overall European scenario construction they have relevance for other situations as well.

(e) After that there has been an analysis of the possibilities for clustering the 27 scenarios into meaningful clusters. This resulted in 4 overall groups of scenarios at the European level.

(f) The final step was a questionnaire send to experts on the EU-level in order to see whether the strategy-scenario combinations provided a workable and meaningful method for policy makers.

In table 1 we give a list of the revised and improved scenarios of the countries in phase 2 (step 4).

Table 1: **Scenarios phase 2**

1a	Czech Republic	Scepticism to change (scenario I)
1b	Czech Republic	Growth-solidarity (scenario II)
1c	Czech Republic	Growth-competitiveness (scenario III)
2a	United Kingdom	Crisis looms and the big players step in (scenario I)
2b	United Kingdom	Ad hoc responses to global pressures (scenario II)
2c	United Kingdom	The free market approach to competitiveness on course (scenario III a)
2d	United Kingdom	A social partnership approach to competitiveness develops (scenario III b)
3a	Luxembourg/Belgium	Controlled globalisation (scenario I)
3b	Luxembourg/Belgium	Regulation (scenario II)
3c	Luxembourg/Belgium	Proximity of training (scenario III)
4a	Slovenia	Economic and social crisis (scenario I)

4b	Slovenia	Slow and steady (controlled) growth (scenario II)
4c	Slovenia	Economic growth and flexibility (scenario III)
5a	Estonia	Good start (scenario I)
5b	Estonia	Splitting into two (scenario II)
5c	Estonia	Dissolving (scenario III)
6a	Austria	Internationalisation (scenario I)
6b	Austria	Harmonization (scenario II)
6c	Austria	Regionalisation (scenario III)
7a	Greece	Complete domination of the market and increased inequalities on multiple levels (scenario I)
7b	Greece	Individual and selective responses to the effects of globalisation (scenario II)
7c	Greece	Competitive economy- lifelong learning-new dimensions in social policy (scenario III)
8a	Poland	Limited development/ad hoc adjustments (scenario I)
8b	Poland	Growth, Cooperation and competition (scenario II)
9a	Germany	From the dual to the plural system of vocational education (scenario I)
9b	Germany	Work process related and shaping oriented vocational education (scenario II)
9c	Germany	Revaluation of formal education and lifelong learning (scenario III)

In step 5 the 27 scenarios are clustered into four groups on the bases of the following exercise. The scores of the 27 scenarios on the economic and social dimensions are placed in a graph. This resulted in 4 theoretical clusters.

Cluster 1 Europe and education: always ahead
This a scenario in which the economic development is piping the tune, social aspects are following this development with a certain distance. Economic restructuring is a prime mover in society.

Cluster 2 Europe and education: rising high
This is a scenario in which Europe develops itself widely in both economic and socials spheres. The economic and social domains are encouraging each other and create a synergic effect.

Cluster 3 Europe and education: still together
This is a scenario in which there is downward development in Europe. Maybe not a crisis but certainly not a road ahead. Economic and social aspects are nevertheless in pace with each other although at a low level of development.

Cluster 4 Europe and education: it's worth it
This is a scenario in which the economic development is lagging behind the social infrastructure. Although the economic development might be at a relatively low level the general feeling in Europe is that aspect as social inclusion, migration and integration do require that social emphasis.

The European Commission's Forward Studies Unit developed in 1999 scenarios on overall European policy development. They arrived at five scenarios, which they termed 'coherent, concerted and plausible images', representing the spectrum of possibilities, factors and players which could in future play a crucial role.
- Scenario 1, 'The Triumph of the Market'
- Scenario 2, 'A Hundred Flowers'
- Scenario 3, 'Divided Responsibilities'
- Scenario 4, 'The Developing Society'
- Scenario 5, 'The Turbulent Neighbourhood'

If we compare the two sets of scenarios (table 2), we can see the overlap between them. In some cases two of our scenarios fit the description of the European commission scenarios.

Table 2: **European Commission scenarios and Cedefop/ETF compared**

EUROPEAN SCENARIOS	SCENARIOS OF THIS PROJECT
Triumph of the market	Europe and education: always ahead
Divided responsibility	Europe and education: it's worth it/rising high
A hundred flowers	Europe and education: still together
The developing society	Europe and education: rising high/it's worth it
The turbulent neighbourhood	Europe and education: still together

Strategies

The countries also developed country specific strategies and clustered them. These national clusters were however not comparable. In order to reach a comparable point of view we regrouped the strategies in 4x2 categories. We based these categories on a mixed state/market model. We called that the model of market coordination by government. The government plays a determining role in the coordination of the market. Demand and supply must be in proportion in this market situation. Therefore information is a necessary condition. A market can't exist by itself, it must be created and the government should act as market supervisor. This is graphically presented in figure 1.

Figure 1: **The model 'Market coordination by government'**

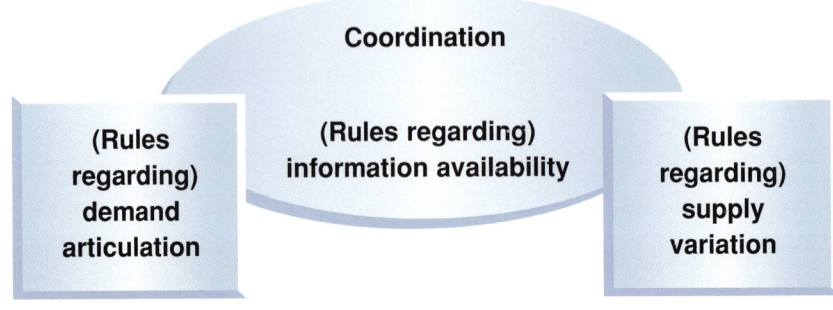

The clusters are listed below.
I (Rules regarding) demand articulation
1 Modern worker strategy
2 Individual is financially responsible for own training strategy

II (Rules regarding) supply variety
1 Flexible providers/networks of providers strategy
2 More training within firms/learning organizations strategy

III (Rules regarding) information available to clients, students and firms
1 Forecasting strategy
2 Transparency/availability strategy

IV Coordination of the process and interventions by market failure
1 Monitoring (quality control, free entrance of new providers, counter monopolies) strategy
2 Protection strategy

The country strategies are classified in the clusters mentioned above. Often, the country strategies aren't equally divided over the categories. There can be several strategies in one category or even no strategies at all. It depends on what's considered important by a country. Some categories are more 'popular' than others. Cluster IV.1 (coordination; monitoring) for example contains only three strategies, while 26 strategies are placed in cluster I.1 (demand; modern worker) and IV.2 (co-ordination; protection). It's possible that certain clusters are more important than others, but it's also possible that the countries didn't take into consideration every aspect. The skewness of the popularity of strategies gives an insight in what might be missing as far as strategies concerned.

Robustness

We can never really predict the future, so the best strategies are strategies that are relevant in all, or at least in more than one, scenario(s). These strategies are called robust. Each project team worked out the robustness for their strategies vis-à-vis the scenarios used in their country. Every country used different strategies which made it hard to make general conclusions about the robustness. One way to com-pare the robustness of the strategies, is to re-

cluster the strategies and then look at the robustness of the clusters. The strategies were clustered in the 4x2 categories mentioned earlier. The average of the robustness of the strategies in a cluster, is the robustness for the cluster as a whole. The robustness can vary between 1-3.
 1 = least robust
 2 = quite robust
 3 = very robust

Table 3: **Robustness overall**

CLUSTER OF STRATEGIES		ROBUSTNESS
Demand	Modern worker strategy	1.77
	Individual is responsible for own training strategy	2.00
Supply	Flexible providers/networks of providers strategy	1.88
	More training within firms/learning organisations strategy	2.00
Information	Forecasting strategy	2.33
	Transparency/availability strategy	2.40
Coordination	Monitoring strategy	1.50
	Protection strategy	2.15

When we put the scores on robustness together in one table, one can see that the forecasting strategy and the transparency/availability strategy are the most robust strategies. They have a score of respectively 2.33 and 2.40. The protection strategy is also robust with a score of 2.15. The least robust cluster of strategies is the monitoring strategy. It has a score of 1.50. Also relatively low on robustness is the modern worker strategy. With a score of 1.77 it's below average. Most scores are above 2.00.

Relevant EU-level actors on strategy and scenario action

When we look at the results of the questionnaire we've sent to relevant EU-level stakeholders, we can conclude that some scenarios are considered to be more relevant for the EU policy makers than others. Europe and education: always ahead and Europe and education: rising high are the most seen as frames of reference for EU policy makers. More than half the respondents believe that those two scenarios are most used as a reference by policy makers.

Within these scenarios we can allocate strategies that could be useful. According to the respondents the following strategy elements are needed in the EU policy in the field of training and LLL: the transparency strategy, the flexible (networks of) providers strategy, the modern worker strategy and the more training within firms strategy. When we compare these results to the coordination-by-government-market model (see figure 1) it can be seen that the coordination category is under-represented. The transparency strategy belongs to the information cluster, the modern worker strategy to the supply cluster and the flexible providers and more training within firms strategy to the demand cluster. This means that none of the strategies in the coordination cluster is often mentioned. Apparently the respondents don't value the monitoring or the protection strategy a lot. There's a preference for the demand cluster. Both strategies in this cluster are considered useful.

Earlier we stated that robust strategies are the best strategies. They can be used in more than one scenario and are thus 'safer' than strategies that are only appropriate in one scenario. Those results can be found in table 3. What we're interested in now, is to see whether the strategies that are needed in the overall EU policy are also the most robust strategies. In the table below the popularity of the strategies is compared to their robustness. A strategy is popular when many respondents believe it should be implemented, when they consider it important. The robustness varies between 1-3. 1 = least robust 2= quite robust 3= very robust.

Table 4: **Strategies: scores and robustness**

STRATEGY	SCORE	ROBUSTNESS
Transparency	37	2.40
Flexible providers	35	1.88
Modern worker	31	1.77
More training within firms	31	2.00
Individual is financially responsible	13	2.00
Protection	13	2.15
Forecasting	11	2.33
Monitoring	3	1.50

The transparency strategy is considered important and it's a very robust strategy with a score of 2.40. In fact, it's the most robust strategy. It would be a good decision to implement this strategy. The more training within firms is also an important and robust strategy. The other 2 strategies the respondents thought were needed are less robust. The forecasting strategy is a very robust strategy, but the respondents don't mention this strategy a lot when it comes to strategies that are needed in EU policy.

Method

The scenario method can be a powerful planning tool, the future being unpredictable it can at least help to give some orientation and guideline to future alternatives. Creating scenarios requires people to question their basic and broad assumptions about the way the world works so they can anticipate decisions that might be missed or denied otherwise and verify whether their thinking retains all potential trends and necessary elements. It makes policy makers and practitioners aware of alternatives. Scenarios help to look beyond the present situation and current developments. That's one of its strengths. This method can also be recommended, be-cause it's capable for a high degree of adaptation to different more or less complex environments so it can be useful in a wide range of settings. The scenario method offers a base for a structured debate between researchers and policy makers or different kind of stakeholders with a wide range of different interests which may all be legitimate but also highly contradictory.

The participating countries conceive the scenario project as an interesting, valuable learning experience. It's a method with enormous potential, but in case of VET it still needs some adjustments. The partner institutes made suggestions of what could be done better/differently. It was almost unanimously stated that a continuation of the project is necessary. The experiences of this project could be used for a series of follow up projects in the EU-countries and the ascending countries and at the EU level as such. The outcomes of this project may back and bring forward at least at a certain extent the efforts made by policy makers and officials of the governments and EU-institutions and agencies within the European employment strategy, the discussion of new concrete objectives for education and training and on the chances and dangers linked to a certain 'Europeanisation' of education and training policies in the light of the forthcoming discussions on the European identity and constitution of parliaments, European institutions and heads of states and governments in the year 2004.

1. Scenarios and strategies

'(...) the eye cannot see what it is not prepared to see. So the mind cannot perceive the patterns of events in the world that it is not prepared to see. Scenarios are tools for preparing the mind to see the future as it unfolds in front of you.' Peter Schwartz (1991)

Strategic planning is considered of increasing importance for organisational management as well as for policy makers in various sectors, including education and training. Strategic planning takes into account the ever-changing environment, objectives and different actors. One way of planning more effective strategies is by means of scenarios. In that sense, scenarios are not an end in itself, but a means to open minds towards better thinking about the future and towards the best possible strategies.

In this chapter we will first examine strategic planning in vocational education and training and the actors involved. Next we will give a general introduction to scenario construction and its different approaches. We proceed with some remarks concerning the strengths and weaknesses concerning the scenario method. This chapter is concluded with some examples of scenario projects.

1.1. Strategic planning in VET and LLL

According to Haselhoff and Piëst (1992), a strategy is a consistent ensemble of essential principles for the behaviour of an organisation or a system as a whole in its environment. What is at issue is the position of the system vis-à-vis the environment. A relatively peaceful environment will call for different strategies than a turbulent environment. An essential factor in strategic planning therefore is the focus on the environment (cf. De Leeuw, 1988). What lies in store in the environment and how can the system react to it? Strategic management is assuming responsibility for the maintenance and improvement of a relatively independent position vis-à-vis the environment. It also includes maintaining and developing capacities that are required to make any adjustments to the organisation (cf. De Leeuw, 1988).

We can easily apply this definition to vocational education and training systems as well. The relation between VET systems and their contexts do change in a dynamic environment, but there is a reasonable degree of predictability in the direction of change.

In the control-orientated interpretation of the environment, all those involved in the VET system explicitly use the existing opportunities to control or influence certain bodies in the environment. We can break down the control into the main kinds of bodies that are involved, i.e. resource suppliers, groups of clients, competitors and regulatory bodies.

Control of resource suppliers is concerned with financial and material matters, but also with the access to trainee placements and training resources. Within some VET systems the maintenance of a fixed input of students for example, implies a permanent relation with the client group concerned. Control of competitors can take place in a variety of ways: driving competitors out of the market, price agreements, and the formations of cartels. It is more difficult for individual VET providers to influence the regulators, but should they form an association of VET providers, they are by no means powerless. The formation of networks can be an attractive way to control the environment.

An ideal type model of strategic planning consists of a number of stages: the arrangement of the drawing up process, the environmental analysis, the internal analysis of strong and weak points, the recognition of alternatives, the objectives, the chosen strategy, the chosen strategy, and finally the implementation.

The drawing up of strategies can take place in various ways. In the first place, there is an interaction between deliberate and spontaneous strategy formation. Another important element is devoting attention to the execution of former strategies and to the recognition of strategies that have apparently been applied. It is also important to decide what combination of process arrangements is given priority: strong top-down or more bottom-up processes.

The environmental investigation consists of an analysis of a number of social developments that are important for the system, particularly demographic, economic, social and political factors. In this context it is important to analyse the position of present and potential competitors and the position of the 'clients' of vocational education. Questions that need to be answered are: Which elements are taken into account in the environmental analysis? Is an analysis carried out of the general environment or does it focus on a specific area? Does it include national and regional economic developments, demographic developments in national and regional perspective, political developments and cultural developments? Does it tackle competition in the sector? Is there an analysis of the specific task environment (specific target groups and customers, specific support groups)? The analysis of the environment is a kind of diagnosis, particularly in order to determine the strong and weak points of the system.

There are other conceivable output indicators too. A VET system can try to discover its strong and weak points in terms of a variety of result indicators such as qualifications attained, productivity, flow to the labour market, customer satisfaction, staff loyalty and attractiveness for clients.

After these analytical stages of the planning process, the more confrontational stages are reached. The first is a confrontation of the results of the analysis with the current practices. Is there a discrepancy between changes in the environment and what the VET system now stands for? Is a problem to be expected at all? Will continuation of the present functioning of the system continue to match up to what is expected of the institution in the future? Or is the system in danger of becoming significantly detached from the relevant environment in the near future?

Besides the question of content, it is possible to examine a number of formal aspects of the objectives (Krijnen, 1993). Is there recognition of the importance of the formulation of objectives? What objectives are necessary in order to determine whether the VET system works effectively enough and to assess alternative solutions to training problems?

Is the specificity of the formulations of the objectives sufficient with regard to:
- content (concrete, operational, elaborated in terms of curricula);
- standard (unit of measurement, e.g. productivity per full time position, etc.);
- level (how much productivity is required);
- time perspective (period in which the objectives are to be attained)?

It is not only the question of which objectives the system wants to attain that is important. It is also important to examine which strategic alternatives can occur. What are the options and limitations of the VET system? If the system cannot continue as it did in the past, or only partially so, what options does it have? Is the system ripe for expansion or innovation? Are the current training programmes satisfactory? Are they good enough to be offered to other groups as well? Should new educational programmes be made? And if so, for which groups and at what level?

The next stages in the planning process are concerned with the choice of a strategy or justification of a strategy. Questions can occur like: Is competition better than co-operation? Is expansion of the target group better than innovation of the programmes? The choice of strategy must also be reflected in executive aspects. Does the structure require modification? Is a structure based on smaller, independent units the most adequate? How can the strategy be translated in terms of financial policy, staff policy, project policy and so on?

Within the framework of the Advisory Forum of the European Training foundation, an investigation has been carried out in 1998 on the issue of strategies for innovation in vocational education and training within several countries. At a conference, experts from almost 20 countries highlighted the great diversity of VET systems in Europe and the differences in approach and expectations for the future (McDaniel, 1998). Especially in the CEE countries, that experience extensive changes in the economy, the complexity of the desired changes to VET is challenging.

The following table shows the difference between a more classical innovation method and a more advanced approach:

Table 5: **Innovation methods**

PHASE	CLASSIC METHOD	ADVANCED APPROACH
Problem orientation	Government sees/ has a problem	Various parties see/have a problem and discuss it in interaction
Instrument	Legislation as a policy instrument	Policy instrument is and/or contains incentives leading to a win-win relation
Innovation is directed towards	Top management of institution	The level of task execution (teachers)
Implementation	Adaptation of the legislation	Implementation strategy
Evaluation	Seldom	Measuring levels of success for input into new innovative policies

Source: McDaniel, 1998, p.31

The conclusion written in the report on this ETF-project is that because of differences in history, culture and expectations for the future, a single solution to all problems is not available and never will be. However, some common elements were recognised as important contributors to innovative VET systems:
(a) Certain level of autonomy of VET institutions is needed.
(b) Performance relation between funding and executing party could enhance the results of the system.
(c) Involvement of many actors is crucial.

(d) Vet systems should set an example in both the education system as well as society in general.
(e) An issue strongly neglected is innovation in the field of personnel policies as a form of human resource management.
(f) Strategies for implementation should be considered carefully in advance.
(g) The same applies to the conditions accompanying the implementation.
(h) Innovation in VET is not a temporary issue.

1.2. Strategies and actors in VET systems

The strategies for a VET system can be derived from the functions a VET system fulfils. VET systems are expected to contribute to a variety of social sectors. There is the socio-economic sector for which VET systems are expected to enhance the security of subsistence of the students with respect to their future work and income in their professional life. The economic sector: preparing students to employ certain qualifications and competencies and participation in the labour market. The social sector: facilitating social and cultural enrichment, in part as preparation for future democratic civic participation and the integration of newcomers. And finally VET systems are expected to contribute to the cultural sector: contributing to educational and cultural personal enrichment.

These four functions give way to four bundles of strategies.

(a) The first group is called the socio-economic strategies. Are VET systems socio-economically acceptable to influential groups, also internally? Do they perform adequately, and are they flexible in this respect? The main problems in this area concern the VET systems' role in expanding labour participation. Whatever labour participation's economic significance may be, from an educational perspective, raising large groups in an environment where work plays little or no role in daily life is unwise.

(b) The second group of strategies related to the function of VET systems, is the group of the economic strategies. Are VET systems economically acceptable to important groups, also internally? Do they perform adequately, and are they flexible in this respect? VET systems face other problems in this area than in the first category. Here, a long-term perspective of national survival is oriented toward international economic-industrial restructuring. At issue are the options identified by the influential long-term strategies with respect to modernising the country's economic structure by adapting production and services with a high added value. The position of VET systems in the knowledge infrastructure (Organisations for Scientific Research, institutes of technology, universities, junior colleges, innovation centres, in-formation services, contract teaching, corporate consulting, etc.) merit structural improvement.

(c) The third group of strategies is composed of social strategies. Are VET systems socially acceptable, also in internal respects? Do they perform adequately, and are they flexible in this respect? The main problems here regard the role of VET systems in social integration and development. Their role revolves around juvenile issues, educational integration of newcomers, and their importance in major cities. In major cities training institutions stimulate cohesion between decentralised policy sectors, such as care for the elderly, social housing, education, public safety, and care for drug addicts.

(d) Cultural strategies are the fourth and last group of strategies. Are VET systems culturally acceptable, also in internal respects? Do they perform adequately, and are they flexible in this respect? Culturally, the educational sys-tem has a proven track record of preserving culture and stimulating its development. VET systems could improve in this area as well, for example regarding one of the main responsibilities of education like imparting bind-ing values with a tolerance suited to a multi-cultural context.

VET systems operate within a relatively complex field of institutions, groups, administrative organs, governments, companies, and the like - all expecting to benefit from the system. The actors concerned ('stakeholders', support groups, and constituents) can be identified in various ways, based on degree of activity, based on formal positions, on positions in the public opinion, the degree of involvement in activities or based on the importance by virtue of age, ethnicity, religion, gender, etc.

Classifying these support groups or actors can be done in several ways as well. We subscribe to the following procedure of classification (Mintzberg 1994, cf. also Mitroff 1983):

- providers of resources (central government, local government, the employment office, temporary employment agencies, companies, individuals);
- employees (educational, administrative, and support staff, both organised and independent);
- clients (pupils, students, beneficiary companies, and institutions);
- competitors (VET providers, private programmes);

- partners (other VET providers, regional support groups, professional organisations);
- regulating authorities (Ministry of Social Affairs, other ministries, court decisions);
- supervisory authorities (inspectorate, support groups, competent authorities).

Support groups are not isolated entities. A given stakeholder's quality is influenced by those of the other stakeholders or the entire system of actors. Contradictions between actors' wishes are commonplace in education. By nature vocational education and training has different functions, as described earlier, resulting in various interests of its stakeholders. The different interest positions lead to a veritable tug of war: some demand more job-specific training for entering the workforce; others require lasting preparation in areas outside their profession in anticipation of an increasingly precarious career.

Not all constituents consistently require the same measure of service. Most importantly, coalitions must arise between support groups. This dominant coalition will play a major role in the effectiveness of strategies. Stakeholders and support groups enable a VET system to modify objectives and to formulate new ones, to acquire appropriate means, to allocate resources to the right organisational components and to avoid conflicts between actors (Mitroff, 1983).

We propose to use scenarios to develop and improve strategies, by means of planning and strategic discussion. This means looking at strategies in a different way from the still very common rationalistic approach to decision-making (Van der Heijden 1997, p.4). The underlying thought of the rationalistic approach is that there is only one best answer. Scenario planning however starts with the idea of the unknowable uncertainty and (therefore) that there is no best strategy: what seems best today, could be less successful tomorrow. There is no yes or no decision in scenario planning.

1.3. Scenario construction

The use of scenarios is not predicting the future (what will happen), but exploring the future (what could happen).

Scenarios are not only being constructed in the business community, also research institutes, (local) governments and international organisations are working with scenario planning. Does this perhaps have to do with the turn of the century? Are we more concerned with or interested in the future compared to previous decennia? Or is the popularity of scenario planning to be explained from the fact that the scenario methodology adds something significantly new to the practice of strategic planning and policymaking? Perhaps we have more need now than ever before to make use of a method, which at least can give us the idea of controlling the future?

Scenarios can be powerful planning tools simply because the future is unpredictable. Unlike traditional forecasting, scenarios also embrace qualitative perspectives and the potential for sharp discontinuities that econometric models exclude. Consequently, creating scenarios requires people to question their broadest assumptions about the way the world works so they can anticipate decisions that might be missed or denied (Global Business Network [GBN], homepage).

Building useful scenarios is balancing between what we can expect and fantasy. A scenario should not be build solely on knowledge that we already have, nor on knowledge that cannot be integrated (science fiction). Van der Heijden calls it the crux of the scenario approach that it makes use of insights and knowledge in 'the zone of proximal development'. This is a concept introduced by Vygotsky indicating that an individual's disorganised tacit knowledge becomes meaningful as a result of social interaction (1997, p.8).

To introduce the scenario method, first let us look at some definitions. The Global Business Network (GBN), one of the leading organisations in the field of scenario planning, describes a scenario as follows: 'A scenario is a tool for ordering one's perceptions about alternative future environments in which today's decisions might play out. In practice, scenarios resemble a set of stories, written or spoken, built around carefully constructed plots. Stories are an old way of organising knowledge, and when used as planning tools, they defy denial by encouraging -in fact, requiring- the willing suspension of disbelief. Stories can express multiple perspectives on complex events; scenarios give meaning to these events' (GBN 1999, homepage).

Michael Porter (in Ringland, 1985, p.2) defines a scenario as 'an internally consistent view of what the future might turn out to be - not a forecast, but one possible outcome.' Others, like Van der Heijden, see the scenario planning primarily as a strategic planning method (1996, p.7): 'scenario planning distinguishes itself from other more traditional approaches to strategic planning through its explicit approach towards ambiguity and uncertainty in the strategic question. The most fundamental aspect of introducing uncertainty in the strategic equation is that it turns planning for the future from a once-off episodic activity into an ongoing learning proposition.'

Ringland (p.2) too, looks at scenarios within the context of strategic planning: a scenario is 'that part of strategic planning which relates to the tools and technologies for managing the uncertainties of the future'.

No scenario is ever seen as probable; the probability of any scenario ever being realised is vanishingly small. It's not accuracy that's the measure of a good scenario; the more appropriate measures are:
- plausibility (telling the story about getting from here to there in a rational fashion),
- internal self-consistency and
- usefulness in decision making.

(GBN, homepage).

We add three more characteristics or measures.
- Scenarios are plural; there is not one scenario, since the future can take many shapes.
- They are hypothetical; the factors in the scenarios might relate to each other in different ways.
- And scenarios are holistic; the emphasis is not on separate relationships between variables but on the wholeness, the Gestalt (shape) of certain futures.

We can conclude that scenarios, the narrative structures about the future, are not an aim of the process but a means by which a group of people, whether in a business, non-profit environment or local or international setting, will be better equipped to talk about the consequences of what the future might bring and about the best way to respond to that in terms of strategies.

Scenarios have been used in planning since the 50s. The introduction of scenario planning as a method in the social and economic sciences is generally attributed to the RAND Corporation. Especially experts in national defence at RAND developed scenarios for different army contexts. RAND's Hermann Kahn adopted the term 'scenario', because he liked the emphasis it gave, not so much on forecasting, but on creating a story or myth about the future. In 1967 he published the book 'The Year 2000', in which he describes scenarios as a narrative description of hypothetical relations between events to draw attention to causal relations and decision moments (Kahn, 1967).

Kahn founded the Hudson Institute in the mid-1960's, specialising in looking further into the future to help plan for changes in society. At this point corporate sponsors were sought, which resulted in the introduction of scenario planning in different companies, including in Royal Dutch Shell. This company contributed considerably to the methodology of scenarios by connecting scenarios to their strategic planning. From 1969 to 1970 a project was carried out, called Horizon Year Planning, in which Shell companies around the world were asked to look forward to 1985. The oil price had been based on seemingly predictable factors of demand and supply, which were assumed to be predetermined. When a scenario was constructed that described that oil prices would unexpectedly rise, this idea was considered almost inconceivable. When, however, in 1973 the oil price did rise un-expectedly, Shell was able to act quickly. This success stimulated more and more companies to adopt the scenario method.

When recession began in the 80s, the use of scenarios decreased. Some of that could be attributed to the fact that the method became used over-simplistically, with confusion between forecasts and scenarios, which gave scenario planning a bad name. The 90s showed a renewed interest in scenario planning, with an emphasis on the use it can have on the strategic planning (Ringland, p.9 ff.).

For a long time regular predictions were popular, based on extrapolations of existent developments. Now less trust is put in this approach. Scenario planning was introduced in the business world to help anticipate specific threats from changes outside of the control of companies. Especially when studying social systems, the reality is very complex. Even without specific threats, scenario planning is now used to help instigate better strategic choices.

Over the years many different ways of conduction scenario research have been developed, differing both in methodology as well as in objective. An essential distinction in the way one can construct scenarios is the so-called prospective or projective way (Van Doorn & Van Vught, 1981). When constructing prospective scenarios, the present is the point of departure from which one systematically works towards the future. By doing so one can construct desirable futures. The projective way on the other hand, starts from the future and works back towards the present. This approach explicitly assumes an 'openness' of the future and results in constructing possible in stead of desirable futures. In this approach one does not build desirable scenarios, but one tries to come up with actions or strategies that will possibly bring about the desired situation.

Figure 2: **Projective scenario development**

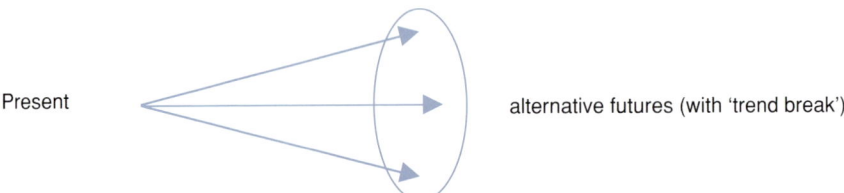

Figure 3: **Prospective scenario development**

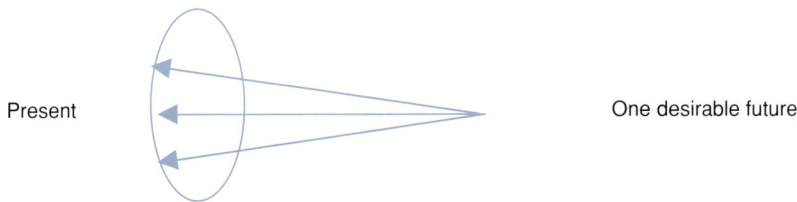

Present   One desirable future

Huss & Honton identified three categories of scenario planning methods in use by 1987, showing different aims of the procedure (Ringland, pp. 24-27):
- The first method is called Intuitive Logics and is used by Royal Dutch Shell and SRI. It was developed by one of the leading futurist Pierre Wack. Its essence is to change the way people think about the future. 'The emphasis is on creating a coherent and credible set of stories of the future as a 'wind tunnel' for testing business plans or projects, prompting public debate or in-creasing coherence.'
- The second category of scenario planning method is the Trend-impact Analysis. This method is mainly concerned with the effects of trends. The difference with other scenario planning methods is that they are usually more orientated towards looking for the unexpected, i.e. what could upset the trends.
- The third method is the 'Cross-impact analysis' and is about identifying a large number of trends that will influence decision making but each other as well. This is done by using a computer to sort through the different combinations of probabilities and cross-impacts. It is therefore a more technical approach (similar to econometric approaches), which can make the interrelationships between a large number of variables visible.

Another method mentioned by Thomas F. Mandel in 'the Strategic Management Handbook' (Ringland, pp. 21-23) is the so-called 'Morphological approach'. In this approach a large number of scenarios is developed to review before making decisions. It starts with possible assigning possible conditions to selected driving forces. Then all the different combinations of each of these factors are put together, creating a tree of scenarios that grows into more and more branches. This method will describe many specific alternatives, but perhaps too many to be able to develop strategies on them.

The Intuitive Logic approach is one that is widely used today. But even within this method there are three different ways of constructing scenarios after the basic trends and data has been gathered. Van der Heijden (1997) subdivides the way of developing a number of internally consistent story lines (scenarios) into inductive, deductive and incremental method:

'In the inductive method the approach builds step by step on the data available and allows the structure of the scenarios to emerge by itself. The overall framework is not imposed; the story lines grow out of the step by step combining of the data. In the deductive method the analysis attempts to infer an overall framework to start with, after which pieces of data are fitted into the framework, wherever they fit most naturally. (…) A third way of developing scenarios I call the incremental method. This approach aims lower and is useful if the client team still needs to be convinced that the scenario approach offers the opportunity to enhance the strategic conversation. In situations where scenario planning is not yet embedded in the thinking style of the organisation the client team may still be strongly attached to an 'official future', a shared forecast that is implicitly the basis of all thinking about strategy. For a client the first steps on a scenario planning road are easier if the official future is used as a starting point, from which the scenarios make excursions into surrounding territory' (Van der Heijden 1997, p. 196).

We will look more closely at the incremental method. Despite its story-like qualities, scenario planning follows systematic and recognisable phases. The process is highly interactive, intense, and imaginative. It begins by isolating the decision to be made, rigorously challenging the mental maps that shape one's perceptions, and hunting and gathering information, often from unorthodox sources. The next steps are more analytical: identifying the driving forces (social, technological, environmental, economic, and political); the predetermined elements (i.e., what is inevitable, like many demographic factors that are already in the pipeline); and the critical uncertainties (i.e., what is unpredictable or a matter of choice such as public opinion). These factors are then prioritised according to importance and uncertainty. The two most important and uncertain developments are then selected, described as extremes on a continuum and crossed within a matrix (see table 6).

Table 6: **Scenario matrix**

	KEY FACTOR 1 (-)	KEY FACTOR 1 (+)
Key factor 2 (-)	Scenario I	Scenario II
Key factor 2 (+)	Scenario III	Scenario IV

These exercises culminate in three or four carefully constructed scenario 'plots.' If the scenarios are to function as learning tools, the lessons they teach must be based on issues critical to the success of the decision. Only a few scenarios can be fully developed and remembered, and each should represent a plausible alternative future, not based on a best case, worst case or most likely criteria. Once the scenarios have been fleshed out and woven into a narrative, the team identifies their implications and the leading indicators to be monitored on an ongoing basis.

When some of the scenarios have been fleshed out, the next step is to try to find strategies that provide relevant actions within the alternative futures, by checking or assessing what implication each strategy has in each scenario. The objective is to look for a robust strategy: a strategy that performs well over the full range of scenarios considered. One way of evaluating the strategies is to integrate the scenarios and strategies in a matrix (see table 7). This way it is clearly illustrated that all strategies need to be evaluated within all scenarios.

Table 7: **Strategies & scenarios**

	SCENARIO I	SCENARIO II	SCENARIO III
Strategy 1	Does this strategy 'fit' this scenario?	Does this strategy 'fit' this scenario?	Does this strategy 'fit' this scenario?
Strategy 2	Does this strategy 'fit' this scenario?	Does this strategy 'fit' this scenario?	Does this strategy 'fit' this scenario?
Strategy 3	Does this strategy 'fit' this scenario?	Does this strategy 'fit' this scenario?	Does this strategy 'fit' this scenario?
Strategy 4	Does this strategy 'fit' this scenario?	Does this strategy 'fit' this scenario?	Does this strategy 'fit' this scenario?

At this stage it is again important to resist the temptation of developing preferences for specific scenarios and actions as the most likely or most wanted. Ultimately, when we can adopt a robust strategy today, we will be better prepared for several of the alternative tomorrows.

2. Design of the project

2.1. Design of phase 1

Objective and participants

The scenario project aims to develop scenarios that can serve as tools to develop strategies for vocational education and training systems in their economic-technological, employment-labour and training-knowledge environments. The strategic dialogue that follows can serve as a basis for advising the decision makers in the respective Member States, applicant Central Eastern European States and through-out Europe.

We are aiming to develop alternative scenarios for the future, which can serve as tools for strategic discussion and planning. To reach this goal the project is de-signed to gather data from selected groups of experts in ten European countries concerning trends in the environment of VET systems and elements of possible strategies regarding VET systems. This data is analysed to find the differences and similarities between the countries and groups of experts, as well as finding overall outcomes on a European level. The objective is to gather quantitative data, based on questionnaires, as well as qualitative data, based on interviews and discussion.

Applied to this project and our objectives, the scenarios have the following aim:

Scenarios are useful in catering for changes that are hard to detect. The scenarios developed within this project can identify early warning signals, which identify and continually reassess critical issues of European significance.

- They help in the determination of the robustness of the qualities of vocational education and of the vocational education policy system.
- They help to instigate better strategic options.
- They assess the risk/profit profile of each strategic option in the light of uncertainties.
- They communicate messages within the system, in a way the stakeholders of the VET-systems can learn from each other.

The participating countries and institutes were selected by (and in agreement with) Cedefop and the European Training Foundation (ETF), while taking into account significant variations in their systems of vocational education and training and in different educational, training and labour market arrangements.

In each country, one partner institute performed the research in the respective country in close co-operation with the scientific and technical co-ordination unit in Amsterdam and under the general co-ordination of both Cedefop in Thessaloniki and ETF in Turin. The Max Goote Expert Center (MGK) of the Universiteit van Amsterdam is responsible for the scientific and technical co-ordinating tasks throughout the project, which includes developing the methodology, supervising the communication and sub-contracting. Whereas the partner institutes were responsible for the re-search in their country, the MGK carried out the analysis at the European level. The partners are:

Table 8: **Partners**

CEDEFOP	EUROPEAN TRAINING FOUNDATION (ETF)
Austria Institut für Berufs- und Erwachsenen Bildungsforschung (IBE) – Universität Linz	Czech Republic Research Institute of Technical and Vocational Education (VÚO?) – Praha
Germany Institut für Technik & Bildung (ITB) – Universität Bremen	Estonia Estonia Education Forum and Technical University – Tallinn
Greece Labour Institute GSEE – ADEDY – Athens	Hungary* Institute of Sociology and Social Policy (ELTE), Eotvos Lorand University – Budapest
Luxembourg/Belgium Etudes et Formation – Luxembourg	Poland BKKK - Cooperation Fund, Task Force for Training and Human Resources – Warszawa
United Kingdom Institute of Education – University of London Qualifications & Curriculum Authority – London	Slovenia Faculty of Social Sciences, University of Ljubljana – Ljubljana

* Hungary didn't complete phase 2. They left the project in January 2001 and there are no Hungarian data available for this phase.

Scenario planning approach

Peter Schwartz (op cit.) said: 'scenario making isn't rocket science'. As long as science doesn't provide us with a theoretical framework, we will have to design our model or approach on the basis of common sense and empiricism. We need to make a model that leads to a systematic description of alternative futures. The basis of our model first of all comes from primary and secondary data, and the development of a questionnaire and/or exploitation of statistical data. Another part of the model is the combination of qualitative data (how and why of a phenomenon) and quantitative data (frequency and distribution of a phenomenon) by using respective interviews/discussions and the questionnaire.

Concerning the various scenario methods as described in the previous chapter, the approach we will use here could be described as projective and related to the Intuitive Logic method. Summarising, this means that we start from the future and work back towards the present. In this approach one does not build desirable scenarios, but one tries to come up with actions or strategies that will possibly bring about the desired situation. The key is to change the way people think about the future, emphasising on creating a coherent and credible set of stories of the future as a 'wind tunnel' for testing strategies.

We will take into account the method described by Van der Heijden, which is use-ful in situations where a scenario building is not embedded in the thinking and where the potential users may still be rather attached to an official future; a shared forecast that is implicitly the basis of all thinking about a strategy. We therefore chose to include the official future in the starting point, from which the scenarios make excursions into surrounding territory.

This approach has been worked out in the following model and stages.

Design and Data collection
(a) Defining the scope and the key question;
(b) Identifying the major stakeholders;
   (i) identifying basic trends;
   (ii) identifying basic strategy elements.

Data analysis
(c) Identifying key uncertainties, driving forces;
(d) Classification of the main developments according to importance and uncertainty. Aim is to find the two major developments that are the most important as well as most uncertain;
(e) Constructing initial scenario themes and matrices.

Discussion
(f) Developing scenarios

General themes emerge from the simple scenarios and from checking them. Al-though the trends appear in all the scenarios, they can be given more or less weight or attention in different scenarios. Because a scenario is a story, they should be given a title. The titles and themes are focal points around which to develop and test the scenarios. At this stage not all scenarios need to be fleshed out.

(g) Checking for consistency and plausibility

There are at least three tests of internal consistency:
- Are there trends compatible within the chosen time frame?
- Do the scenarios combine outcomes of uncertainties that indeed go together? (For example, zero inflation and full employment don't go together)
- Are the major stakeholders placed in positions they do not like and can change?

Follow-up
(h) Evolving toward decision scenarios and robust strategies

Next we retrace the previous steps and see if the learning scenarios and strategies address the real issues facing the European VET-system. To test if the final scenarios are any good, they should be:
- Relevant. To have impact, the scenarios should connect directly with the mental maps and concerns of the users;
- Internally consistent and perceived as such;
- Archetypal; they should describe generally different futures rather than variations on one theme;
- Describing an equilibrium, or a state in which the system might exist for some length of time.

(i) Strategic conversation.

To develop these scenarios and strategies a strategic conversation should have taken place. 'It is the general conversational process by which people influence each other, the decision taking and the longer term pattern in institutional action and behaviour'(Van der Heijden, p. 239). This conversation should be maintained.

(j) Institutionalisation

'Ultimately the most effective way to ensure institutional effectiveness of the scenario process is for management to make the scenarios part of the ongoing formal decision making process' (Van der Heijden, 1996, p.277 ff.). The scenarios have to become part of the organisation for discussing strategic questions.

Project implementation phase 1
The aim of the investigation and the subsequent data analysis in the first phase of the project are summarised in following questions:
(a) Which trends in the contexts of VET are considered important and/or likely?
(b) What are the strategies considered being relevant?
(c) Who are considered to be the most responsible institutions and actors to take action?

Combining the answers to these three questions, what are alternative futures for VET in Europe and who should take which actions?

To come up with the answers to these questions we asked the opinion of a large number of experts in ten countries (around 200 stakeholders per country). The different steps are listed in the following paragraphs. These include developing the questionnaire, selecting the population, collecting and analysing the data, discussing the outcomes and the follow up.

Developing the questionnaire
The project started in January 1999 with the preparation of the questionnaire, the selection of experts and stakeholders and with methodological work. In January 1999 the Max Goote Expert Center scanned recent literature on VET in different countries to collect a large variety of developments and strategies. Among the sources were several scenario projects like the Dutch scenario-project and the United Nations University's Millennium project. Other sources were provided by important Cedefop and OECD publications. The questionnaires have been developed through several stages. On the basis of this material a first basic draft of a questionnaire was prepared, containing a number of trends and strategies. The first draft was sent to the partner institutes who were asked to revise and complement the list of trends and strategies proposed. By asking all the partners in this project about their own trends they perceived, we collected and included developments that are divergent from the sources retained so far. The objective was to collect a number of common trends that can be recognised within the countries concerned, although the importance or the stages of development may differ. By interaction through e-mail, the various drafts were discussed and revised.

The Max Goote Expert Center constructed new common versions on the basis of this information and a meeting was organised in February 1999, with one representative from each of the countries participating and representatives from the coordination unit, Cedefop and ETF. At the meeting the terminology and formulation of the items were discussed and agreement was reached about the final format and content.

Three different questionnaires were developed, each covering a specific context in which vocational education and training is situated. We called them Context A: Economy and Technology, Context B: Employment and the labour market and Context C: Training, skills and knowledge. With a different accent in each questionnaire we included descriptions of trends on issues like international competition, ICT/innovation, globalisation/regionalisation, local and company development, the flexibility of labour/mobility, demography, knowledge/learning concepts in organisations, (un)employment, social exclusion, access to education and non formal learning.

The division between the contexts/questionnaires is not absolute; there was some overlap. As we assumed that each respondent would fill in only one questionnaire, an overlap of the topics was included to get the views on the same issues from respondents with different backgrounds.

Figure 5 presents a graphic overview of the connection between the contexts, the VET system and strategies.

In each context the respondents were asked to score and comment on the importance and likelihood of 23 trends and the relevance and most important actors of 20 strategy elements. The same strategy elements were divided over the three con-texts. The partners had the opportunity to add a maximum of three trends and three strategy elements to each questionnaire that are aimed at the country specific situation, in addition to the common questionnaires. These added variables were not included in the European data analysis. Finally a number of open questions were added in asking comments on the answers to the trends or strategies.

The list of actors, which would be responsible for implementing strategies, that the respondents could choose from were: EU institutions/agencies, national state, local/regional government, employer associations, trade unions, sectors, (groups of) enterprises, VET providers and individuals.

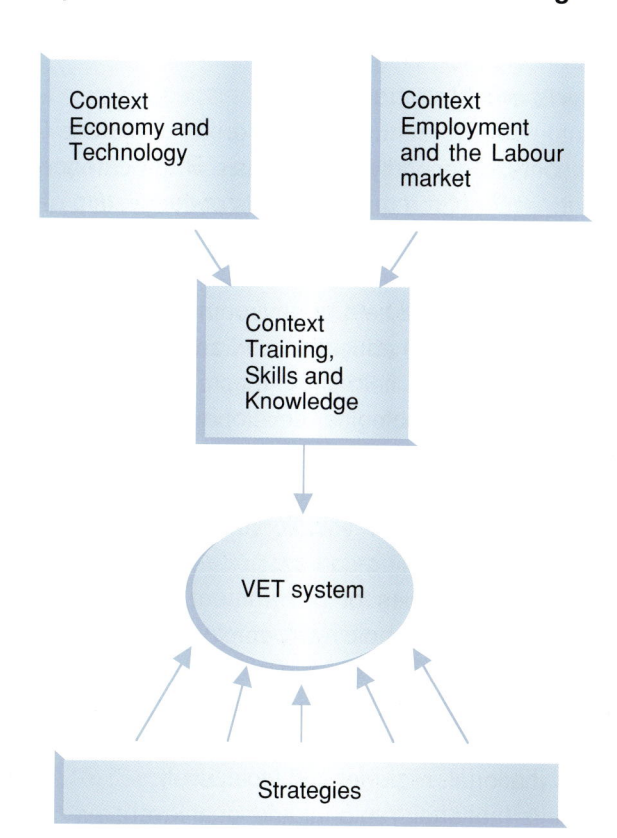

Figure 4: **Conceptual scheme of the contexts and strategies**

The year to focus on by the respondents was the year 2010. The timeframe chosen is therefore around 10 years. It is a time span long enough to include long-term developments, but short enough to be anticipated by looking into the future.

One of the challenges that we encountered drawing up the questionnaires was avoiding falling for the temptation of selecting bland and general trends. There is a tendency, when developing a questionnaire with a large number of people of different backgrounds and nationalities, that the 'direction' of the given statements of the trends (and strategies) risks to follow mostly the mainstream discussion and rather general issues. This was at least to a certain extent the case in this endeavour too. In the first versions we included some items that could be called 'controversial' and focussed at more specific issues, e.g. gender questions, VET in certain branches etc. These were, however, excluded as a result of a consensus-based procedure of developing the questionnaire. This is one of the issues we looked at in the follow up/second phase of the project.

Selecting experts and stakeholders
Within the countries, each team selected a group of experts first on the basis of the relevant context, secondly on the basis of the category of the respondents. Taking into account the three contexts of the system of vocational education and training that were distinguished, the following criteria for selecting the experts were used:
- assumed expertise in the field of environmental changes that may be of importance for vocational education and adult education;
- assumed expertise in the field of the macro determinants, particularly the labour market and technological developments, in relation to vocational education and adult education;
- assumed capacity to formulate motivations concerning future developments that are relevant for vocational education and adult education, including firm-based training courses;
- membership of the circles of government, vocational education, firm-based training courses, employees, employers and the academic world;
- the participants ought to be able to grasp the changes in their field and have a clear picture of what these mean for VET developments.

Experts were then located in the following 10 categories of actors:
- (a) politicians (national, regional and local level);
- (b) civil servants (national, regional and local level);
- (c) enterprises or groups of enterprises;
- (d) employer associations/chamber of commerce;
- (e) employee associations, unions, chamber of labour etc;
- (f) sectoral organisation, professional associations;
- (g) training providers, institutes for VET;
- (h) universities, research institutes;
- (i) consultancy agencies, advisory agencies;
- (j) non-affiliated experts, non-governmental agencies, media..

Data collection
The partner institutes in each country followed a standardised procedure carrying out the questionnaire management and the assessment of national data. The questionnaires were translated within each country into the respective language. The respondents received the questionnaire together with a letter explaining the purpose of the study and a short glossary of terms. In order to protect the data and to en-sure confidentiality of responses, the data were sent

to the Max Goote Expert Center identified only by numbers assigned by the partner institutes.

Approximately 600 experts (200 for each environment/questionnaire) were identified in each country. The response rate differed from one country to another. Some countries decided to present the respondents the three contexts (three sets of questionnaires) altogether. Others sent one questionnaire to each respondent as agreed. Some national teams decided to leave it to the respondent which context to fill in and how many.

This, however, influenced the European sample to a large extent. Hungary for ex-ample received 306 questionnaires back from 120 respondents, whereas Germany mailed one questionnaire directly to about 750 people separately, receiving back 196. For the data processing on European level we decided not to sort on respondent, but on questionnaire. If it would be relevant to know which respondent answered what in different questionnaires, this could be part of the national data analysis.

Analysis

The questionnaires filled in were sent to the technical co-ordination unit to be processed. The Max Goote Expert Center merged the databases and processed the data at the European level. This resulted in a draft comprehensive report with the combined outcomes for the 10 countries. At the same time the partners used their data file to do the initial national data processing and preparation of a draft national report. In order to be able to integrate and compare the results of the analysis some statistical procedures were prescribed. Because of the exploratory nature of the analysis, and the possible differences in the obtained data, the teams were free to perform complementary analysis of their own data, in addition to the overall instructions. The Max Goote Expert Center analysed the data on the European level, with the exception of the written comments, which were analysed and reported by the partner institutes. A translation of these comments was included in most of the national reports, which made it possible to compare the remarks in the European synthesis report. Both reports, of the national and European analysis, served as in-puts for the national seminars, which were held in September/October 1999.

Discussion

The national seminars in the first phase (September-October 1999) were organised by the partner institutes in the participating countries with important stakeholders and experts. Participants mostly came from national and local governments, social partners, VET providers and research institutes. These national seminars focused on the discussion of the method applied, results achieved and described in the draft country report and in the European report, which made it possible to compare the position of the respective country in relation to the others involved. Besides discussing the outcome of the questionnaires and comparing it with the outcomes of the other countries, the objective was to attempt to construct and elaborate first tentative scenario and strategy dimensions on the basis of the qualitative data on this national level and to verify the plausibility and credibility of the outcomes of the investigation.

The results of the discussions were then added to the national report and made avail-able to Cedefop, ETF and the Max Goote Expert Center. On the basis of these ten reports and further data analysis, the co-ordinating unit prepared a synthesis report, describing and comparing the results of the different countries and that of the European analysis. This report forms the basis for the discussion at the European conference organised by Cedefop jointly with ETF and in co-operation with the Greek employment office (OAED) in Athens in January 2000.

Objectives of the European conference are to discuss the initial outcomes of the project and to draw first tentative conclusions for policy and practice of VET at both national and European levels. Furthermore, the follow up of the project to be carried out in the year 2000 has been discussed and prepared.

At the conference representatives of Cedefop, ETF, Max Goote Expert Center and two project managers from each of the participating countries were present. Also invited were 1-2 high level experts/stakeholders from each EU-Member State and from each of the five Accession States, representing public VET bodies as well as national employer and trade union organisations. At the European level representatives from the European Commission and 1 from the European Parliament, 1 from ETUC and 1 from UNICE/CEEP, representing the European Employees' and Employers' organisations were invited.

At the conference, experts from the Max Goote Expert Center together with the national teams presented the main findings on both the national and European levels. The high level stakeholders of the different European countries were asked to comment on these and assist Cedefop and ETF to draw first conclusions on the usefulness of the future scenarios for strategy development and the way they could be further elaborated and developed.

2.2. Design of phase 2

In the beginning of the 2nd phase, the Central Eastern European countries experienced some financial problems. ETF decided there was no additional funding available for 2000. This jeopardized the taking part of some CEE countries in the second phase. MGK reserved 15.000 Euro in total from the previous ETF funding, to distribute among the CEE partners this year. Each country needed to decide whether it was in the financial position to continue participation. The partners concerned (Hungary, Estonia, Slovenia, Poland and the Czech Republic) were asked to inform Cedefop, ETF and MGK before May 31st whether they were able to stay in the project. In the first instance and seen that problems occurred with the financing of the Central Eastern European partners which were solved, however, by ETF quite soon, the start of the 2nd phase was difficult and Hungary finally stepped out for reasons of availability of professional staff at the given time, what the coordinators regretted very much.

Within the second phase the intention was to further develop the scenarios and to notably deepen all aspects linked to strategies, actions and policy measures referring to the alternative scenarios, their ranking in terms of their importance, relevance and robustness. The method was adapted to this end and consisted in the main in intensive interviewing a restricted number of stakeholders and policy-makers. This in-depth analysis lead to a situation, wherein the European level analysis was put into the background and the country-specific appreciations and institutional differences came into the foreground.

Figure 5: **Graphic outline phase 2**

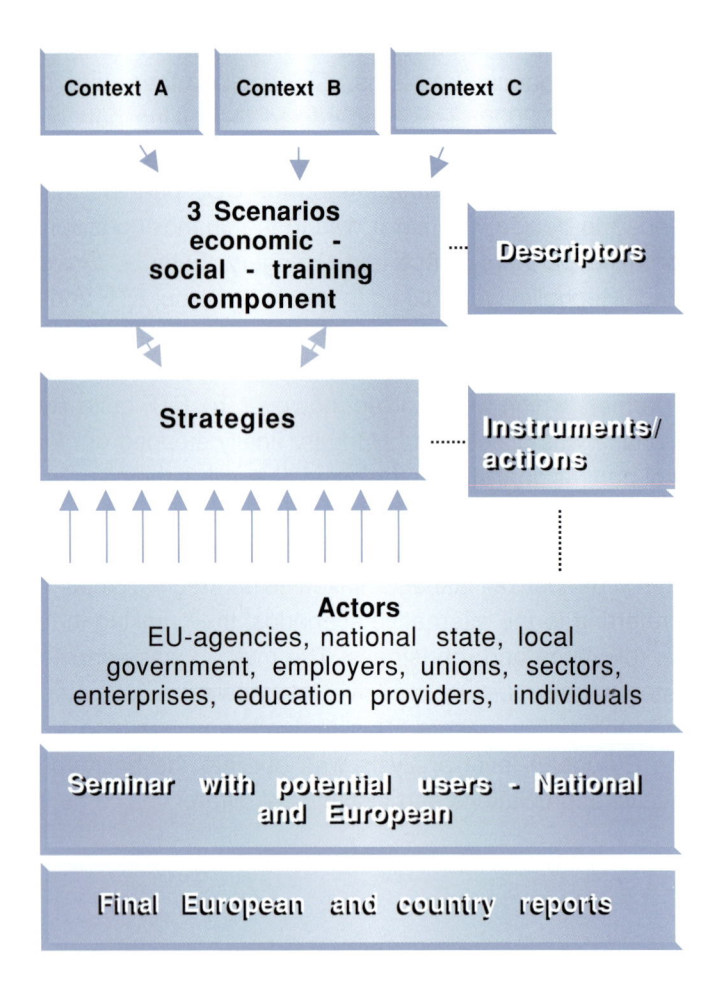

At the beginning of the 2nd phase, a time schedule was made that included the steps to be taken in this phase. This time schedule appeared to be unrealistic. Most steps were postponed a little and some parts of the project even took place a couple of months later than planned. The second phase brought along more work than fore-seen.

Table 9: **Time schedule**

	ACTION	PRODUCT PARTNERS	PRODUCT MGK	DATE
April 2000	Official start phase 2		Proposal work programme	
	Discussing joint framework	Meeting in Brussels		April 14/15
May	Desk research	- Combi-scenarios - Descriptors - Strategies	Revised work programme	
			- Interview guideline - Standardised background information/ documentation	
May-June	Interviews or Workshop scenarios	5-10 transcripts or report workshop		June 15
			- Interview guideline - Standardised background information/ documentation	
July-September	- Elaborating scenarios/ strategies - Interviews strategies	- Paper - +/- 20 transcripts, discussion paper		now: Oct. 15 CZ: Nov. SI: Nov./Dec.
October	Discussing scenarios/ strategies	Workshops		now: Oct./Nov. CZ: Dec. SI: Jan.

December	Integrating results	Draft national report (EN)		now: Dec. 15 CZ: Jan. 10 SI: Jan/Feb H: Mar-Apr 15
January 2001		Final national reports		now: Jan 31 CZ: Jan 31 SI: Feb.
			International outline report on main features	
February	Discussing results	National seminar		CZ: April 5 E: April 2 EL: March 8 PI: April 19 SI: April 24 UK: April 3
March		Final report (EN) (incl. 20-30 p. summary)		now: June/July
			International final report	
April	Presentation results	European Conference at Tallinn		October 1 & 2 2001
	Publication, dissemination			

At the start of phase 2, a time planning was also made by the partner institutes. Three dates had to be fixed. The completion of the draft national report. The draft had to be ready before the meeting in Thessaloniki and send to MGK. The date of the national seminar, and finally the date when the final national report had to be send to MGK. The planning was adjusted several times, because of some unexpected delays.

Descriptors used

Vocational education and training is situated in three specific contexts. Three questionnaires were developed, each covering one of the contexts/dimensions. The three dimensions are:
- economic dimension;
- social-labour dimension;
- training dimension.

For each dimension several descriptors were distinguished. Each dimension had about 17 descriptors (that could be classified into approximately 9 categories). The scenarios had to be written using these descriptors.

Strategies

The strategies are more diverse, because the starting point from the countries is different. The strategies were handled in several ways. The United Kingdom for ex-ample, let people choose two strategies and gave them a third. This way all strategies will be taken into account. They thought people couldn't handle more than three strategies. Furthermore, they put the strategies in past time, like they were al-ready implemented. United Kingdom asked experts how important strategies are across all scenarios using open-ended questions. A strategy can be hard/easy to achieve in a certain scenario.

In order to work with the strategies, they can be:
- clustered;
- ranked (by adequateness, importance, implementation).

Some countries ranked and clustered the strategies, but most partners just clustered them. More information on (the ranking and clustering of) the strategies is included in chapter 6.

Interviews

Most countries did 10-15 interviews.

Austria
11 interviews. The interviews were done by telephone, but they received detailed interview guidelines in advance.

Czech Republic
20 experts. Face by face interviews.

Estonia
The interviewees were invited to the national seminar.

Germany
40 interviews on federal level of high level of experts

Greece
The interviewees could choose between face-to-face interviews and questionnaires. They chose face-to-face interviews.
Luxembourg/Belgium
Poland
Slovenia
United Kingdom
10-11 interviews. They put the strategies in the past as if they were already implemented. They asked experts how important strategies are across the 3 scenarios. Always open ended questions.

National seminars
In this figure an overview is given on the national seminars as they were held in the second phase.

Table 10: **National seminars**

A	**Austria**	March 16 2001 13:30-17:30 Vienna *Cancelled*	Due to a very low participation rate the National Seminar was cancelled and replaced by an internal expert review. The scenarios and strategies (including instruments, actors and measures) were presented and their plausibility, *communicatability*, transferability and robustness were discussed. The topics and results of the discussions required no major changes in the scenarios and strategies.
CZ	**Czech Republic**	April 5 2001 10:00-17:00 Prague	Participants: 21
25 representatives of institutions corresponding in type to the ten categories of respondents we worked with during the whole research where invited to it. The Czech National Report draft version was send together with the invitation. The addressees were asked to read the report, and in particular the parts concerning national scenarios and strategies beforehand and to prepare relevant comments and suggestions for the report adjustment. They also received suggested topics for the discussion. Cedefop was actively participating in this seminar.

Design of the project | 49

EE	Estonia	April 2 2001 10:00-15:00 Tallinn	Participants: 72 The results of the survey were presented and discussed in a national seminar which was held in September 1999 and involved the project's key partners and experts. The seminar focussed on the implications and evaluation of the survey results for the Estonian VET development context as well as on drawing comparisons between Estonia and other countries participating in the survey.
D	Germany	June 13 2001 9:30-16:30 Bonn	*Because of low participation the seminar was postponed, to be held later in the year*
EL	Greece	March 8 2001 14:00-19:00 Athens	Taking part in the meeting of experts in Athens, in addition to researchers from the Institute of Labour (INE)/Greek General Confederation of Labour (GSEE), were a representative of Cedefop, representatives of the social partners' Vocational Training Centres, the agriculture sector, the National Labour Institute, the National Certification Centre for training structures, the Ministry of Labour and the Manpower Employment Organisation (OAED), the Ministry of Education, the Continuing Training Institute, the Pedagogical Institute, Panteion University and the Hellenic Open University.
L/B	Luxembourg/ Belgium	Cancelled	*Most actors were interviewed and a national seminar would have been rather a formality*
PL	Poland	April 19 2001 11:00-16:00 Warszawa	About 20 national experts took part in the seminar. Participants included the representatives of the main vocational education and training 'stakeholders' in Poland and the representatives of Max Goote Institute.
SI	Slovenia	April 24 2001 Ljubljana	Participants: 58 Representatives from unions, VET providers, enterprises, ministry among others. National and international results discussed and compared. Also an attempt was made to further elaborate the scenarios and strategies.

| UK | United Kingdom | April 3 2001 11:00-16:00 London | Participants: 30
There was good representation of government departments (Department for Education and Employment, and Department of Trade and Industry) and agencies (Qualifications and Curriculum Authority, Scottish Qualifications Authority, and the Learning and Skills Agency), as well as university research organisations (Institute of Education, University of Greenwich, University of Warwick). Three representatives of the newly-formed Learning and Skills Councils from the London Area participated, as well as representatives of a number of other organisations and independent consultants. Two constituencies were not well represented, although they had been invited: employers organisations and education training providers (in the latter case, local authorities and FE colleges). Also, throughout the project it had proved difficult to engage the attention of members of parliament. |

3. Constructing the scenarios

3.1. A six step procedure to arrive at the scenarios

The scenarios have been constructed in this project according to a 6-step iterative procedure as follows:

(a) The first was the selection of relevant scenario dimensions on the base of the outcomes of all the 10 participating countries in the first phase of the project. This step resulted in two dimensions for each context. Consequently four provisional scenarios were constructed for each context (with the exception of context C for which 2 times four scenarios were developed).

(b) Based on these groups of four scenarios the participating countries developed for their national situation also provisional scenarios for the different contexts.

(c) Based on the scenarios from step 1 and 2 i.e. the scenarios constructed from the European overall database and the scenarios constructed by each national team the main common characteristics were selected and put together in a sketch for common scenarios to be used by the (by then 9) participating countries in order to improve their provisional scenarios.

(d) This step resulted in improved scenarios for each of the 9 participating countries i.e. in total 27 scenarios. These scenarios have their value and meaning in the national context and because they have been constructed vis-à-vis the overall European scenario construction they have relevance for other situations as well.

(e) After that there has been an analysis of the possibilities for clustering the 27 scenarios into meaningful clusters. This resulted in 4 overall groups of scenarios at the European level.

(f) The final step was a questionnaire send to experts on the EU-level in order to see whether the strategy-scenario combinations provided a workable and meaningful method for policy makers.

We will describe these six iterative steps in the following six paragraphs.

3.2. Provisional scenarios at European level as discussed in phase 1

The major trends identified indicate the importance of public/private partnerships and economic restructuring in order to improve competitiveness, to accompany changes in the workplace and to increasing flexibility/mobility of labour. Important trends directly linked to vocational education are the flexibility of training programmes, a changing role of VET providers, the acceptance of an increasing social dimension/task of education/training policies and an individualisation/decentralisation of training opportunities. On the basis of these factors four provisional scenarios were developed: one for each of the contexts A and B and two for context C.

Clustering of Trends: Context A Economy and technology

An exploratory principal component analysis (PCA) was performed on the 23 trends in each context on the responses of 'importance'. We left out the responses on 'likelihood at this stage, because we wanted to include in the scenarios those developments that the respondents valued most. How certain these developments are, is less important for scenario construction. It will be of course of interest to look whether the trends that show a high score on importance and on uncertainty from the previous paragraph, will be incorporated within the components that result from the PCA.

Since no item presented a normal distribution of answers, we decided to explore the data for possible clusters. Nevertheless, we are also interested whether the five or six themes we incorporated in each of the three questionnaires will show up in the structure of the clusters. We then correlated the factors with the scores for likelihood in order to make a selection for those factors to be used in our attempt at scenario construction.

By performing a PCA we initially looked whether the first factor explained relatively much variance in relation to the other factors. The factors seemed to make enough scale after varimax rotation. The items with a smaller factor loading than .40 were not considered in further analysis since the relation with the concerning factor is too small. An exception is made for those factors that do not have one loading above .40. In those cases we selected the highest score for further analysis. To determine the reliability of the resulting scales we used the Cronbachs' alpha.

In the paragraphs below we will describe the outcomes of the analysis on the European level per context. Then these factors are correlated with the answers on 'likelihood', which provides us with the first provisional scenario dimensions and matrix. Per context the data was analysed further in order to explore the distribution of the scores in each of the countries. This procedure is carried out for con-texts A, B and C and reported in this order below.

After performing a PCA in context A, the following clusters of trends (components) were the result:
- The first component we call 'partnerships in economic development' as it is composed of trends stressing the co-operation between public and private organisations, companies and sector organisations with VET providers.
- Component A2 'restructuring to compete' clusters the trends that are concerned with company structure, restructuring and networks.
- Component A3 'social effects of economic developments' stresses the unpredictable and maybe undesirable effects of economic developments on society.
- Component A4 'competition by innovation' summarises the needs of companies to produce knowledge intensive, be flexible and up to date with ICT developments to be able to compete.
- The final component A5 'impact of economy on wider Europe' is more difficult to interpret, but has to do with the macro effects of the economy on society and Europe in particular.

To select the two dimensions for scenario construction we correlated the scores on these factors with the scores on the same items for likelihood. The two factors that showed the highest correlation, were selected as dimensions for scenario construction. These dimensions can be formulated as two developments going into opposite directions. These are put in a scenario matrix, which results in four scenarios.

Provisional scenarios context A

Table 11: Provisional scenarios context A

	NO OR FEW PARTNERSHIPS	**MANY PARTNERSHIPS**
Weak restructuring for competitiveness	**1. Stagnation** Context in which the economy lingers on and develops no strong linkages with training	**2. Good will, no results** Context in which no strong economic impetus is prevalent, although there are numerous linkages with training providers
Strong restructuring for competitiveness	**3. Short term development** Context in which the economical re-structuring follows its own route with no partnerships from education	**4. Rich development** Context in which the economy is re-structured while at the same time there are many contacts with training providers

The provisional scenarios are given a title and a short description. In each scenario we need to describe the same characteristics of the environment, for example:

What will be the structure of companies in this scenario? What will be the structure of employment sectors? What does the global distribution, patters of competition look like? What can be said about the flow of capital, rate of return on investment? What will be the position of corporate governance and share holders? What level of inequality will be acceptable? How large will the demand for low and intermediate skills be? How will economic growth develop? What will be the demographic situation in terms of ageing, birth rate and ethnic composition? What is the situation of employment and the organisation of labour? Which role does information technology play? What is the role of different actors: European Union, national states, local/regional governments, employers associations, sectors, individual enter-prises, education/training providers, individuals?

By discussing these issues and drawing up the full story about the future, the scenarios will become more alive and useable for strategic dialogue. This activity took place in the second phase of the project.

Clustering of Trends: Context B Employment and the labour market
The components that resulted from the PCA in this context are:
- Component B1 'changes in the workplace'.
  The organisation becomes multicultural, ICT, knowledge management and social skills become more important whereas hierarchies become less important.
- Component B2 'undesirable developments'.
  This component clusters trends like the ageing workforce, unemployment of the young, individualisation, social exclusion, brain drain and polarisation between the high- and low qualified. These are all expected undesirable developments in the labour market.
- Component B3 'mobility of labour' is composed of trends that indicate trends towards mobility of labour and its flexibility, new combinations of work/training, but also migration.
- Component B4 'assurance of (continuing) education' stresses the need for security in education in the form of life long learning, a role for the government, and maintaining good training to combat social exclusion.
- Component B5 'general skills'
  For interpretation we see a high negative score on t02l which indicates a trend towards the need for specific skills. This factor is thus an indicator for the need of broad competencies.

Provisional scenarios context B
Based on the correlation coefficients of the factors with the scores for certain/uncertain we selected the factors 1 and 3 for our initial scenario-construction.

Table 12: **Provisional scenarios context B**

	LOW DEGREE OF MODERNISATION OF THE WORKPLACE	**HIGH DEGREE OF MODERNISATION OF THE WORKPLACE**
Low degree of mobility of labour	**1. Immobility** Context in which organisations stick to traditional patterns and personnel show no eagerness for innovation in their labour pattern	**2. Organisational change** Context in which organisations change their internal structure and processes and at the same time the labour force will not adopt these new practices
High degree of mobility of labour	**3. Flexible workers, inflexible work** Context in which individual workers are able and willing to work and live in new forms while at the same time firms and companies show little innovation in their internal organisation	**4. Synergy** Context in which there is a synergy between organisational and individual modernisation.

As described earlier, these provisional scenarios are just a starting point. We will have to flesh them out. In each scenario we need to describe the same characteristics of the environment, for example:

What will be the internal structure of companies in this scenario? What's the situation of (un-) employment and the organisation of labour? What will be the patterns of employee/employer connections? What will be the structure of employment sectors? What will be the average level of education? How large will the demand for low and intermediate skills be? What types of labour associations will exist and what membership of unions? What level of inequality will be acceptable?

What will be the situation of older people, youngsters at risk, immigrants? What will be the demographic situation in terms of ageing, birth rate and ethnic composition? Which role does information technology play? What is the role of different actors: European Union, national states, local/regional governments, employers associations, sectors, individual enterprises, education/training providers, individuals?

The remaining factors, which are not considered for scenario construction, are factor B2 'undesirable developments', which is clearly a controversial one with a diverse pattern of scoring by the respondents. These undesirable developments are especially seen as important in Greece, followed by Hungary and Slovenia.

Factor B4 on security in social and educational life shows some differences within the group of the EU countries; e.g. the UK scores high on importance whereas Germany scores a below the European level. A relative low score on this factor can be seen in the CEE countries Estonia, Poland and the Czech Republic.

Clustering of Trends: Context C Training, skills and knowledge
The components that resulted from the PCA in this context are:
- Component C1 'flexibility in training programme'
  The demand for general, social and communication skills seem to gain in importance, but will be learned within the company or at least in a programme that is geared to the needs of the individual students.
- Component C2 'changing role of VET providers'
  This factor summarises the changing environment and role of VET providers or training institutions. They have to adapt to regionalisation, decentralisation and a different relation with SMEs.
- Component C3 'the social task of training'
  This factor is composed of trends that stress the social component of vocational training. Older employees, the unemployed as well as groups at risk of social exclusion should also benefit from vocational education and training and perhaps even get special attention.
- Component C4 'individuality'
  The trends included in this factor are concerned with training and the responsibility of the outcome of the education becoming more and more individualised.
- Component C5 'private/non-formal learning'
  This last component is harder to interpret, but seems to represent the changing relationship of formal education with private and non-formal learning. Private sources of funding will become more important; the role of formal education in knowledge management will decline whereas non-formal learning will grow in importance.

In this context we decided, for now, to explore the possibilities a bit more. We therefore look at the first four factors as dimensions for scenario construction, resulting in two scenario matrices.

Provisional scenarios context C

On the base of the correlation between the factors above and the scores for the likelihood we first selected the factors C1 and C2 for the construction of initial scenarios.

Table 13: **Provisional scenarios, context C (I)**

	WEAK DEMAND FOR SOCIAL AND GENERAL SKILLS IN CONJUNCTION WITH IN-COMPANY LEARNING	**STRONG DEMAND FOR SOCIAL AND GENERAL SKILLS IN CONJUNCTION WITH IN-COMPANY LEARNING**
Low contextually responsive VET providers	**1. Traditional inward looking system** Context in which there is no specific need for generic skills and training providers stick to their traditional offerings	**2. Clash between demand and training providers** Context in which there is demand for social and generic skills but no responsiveness from the side of the VET providers
Highly contextually responsive VET providers	**3. Unmet innovation** Context in which providers are willing to innovate and being responsive to new demands, there is however no demand articulated for social or general skills	**4. Demand for social skills met by responsiveness** Context of decentralisation of the training providing structure and high demand for social and general skills

Using factors C3 and C4 provided us with the following scenario matrix.

Provisional scenarios, context C (II)

	TRAINING TO A LESSER DEGREE USED TO PROTECT SOCIALLY CERTAIN GROUPS	TRAINING USED TO A LARGE DEGREE FOR THE PROTECTION OF CERTAIN GROUPS
Training is not so much an individuals responsibility	**1. Fragmentation** Context in which there are no major responsibilities organised for training	**2. State based arrangements** Context in which traditional state-based, social-democratic arrangements prevail
Training is mainly an individuals responsibility	**3. Neo-liberal context** Context in which neo-liberal arrangements are predominant	**4. Individual and collective co-operations** Context in which there are training-based social provisions for specific target groups supplementary to individual responsibilities

In each scenario we need to describe the same characteristics, for example:

What is the relative proportion of school based and firm based training? What is the average percentage firms spend on training? What will be the average level of education? Will teaching be a life time profession? What is the role of teacher-free learning facilities? What is the position of the consumer, the student? How large will the demand for low and intermediate skills be? What education/training provisions will there be for older people, youngsters at risk, immigrants Which role does in-formation technology play in schools? Which role does information technology play outside of schools? What is the role of different actors: European Union, national states, local/regional governments, employers associations, sectors, individual enterprises, education/training providers, individuals?

3.3. Provisional scenarios at national levels

To select the two dimensions for scenario construction in the first phase we correlated the scores on these two factors with the scores on the same items for likelihood. The two factors that showed the highest correlation, were selected as dimensions for scenario construction. These dimensions can be formulated as two developments going into opposite directions. These are put in a scenario matrix, which results in four scenarios. The table below contains of each country the four scenario dimensions in context A and in context B.

Table 15: **Scenarios phase 1**

COUNTRY	SCENARIO DIMENSIONS CONTEXT A	SCENARIO DIMENSIONS CONTEXT B
Austria	Stagnation-Scenario Single-combat Scenario Structures uphold by change Dynamic change	Status-quo-Scenario Scenario: Polarisation Scenario : Open unified society Scenario: Post modern society
Czech Republic		
Estonia	Stagnation Limited, short-term growth Isolated developments Learning economy	Flexible labour market Polarised labour market Unbalanced labour market Limited labour market
Germany	Old national state framework Separated co-existence Defensive networks of enterprises Fragile networks	Neo-taylorism Malleable flexibility Neo-'manchester-capitalism' Learning as a life sentence
Greece	No economic restructuring is taking place. Competition is driven by Knowledge which is been developed in the framework of the existed economic structures. Context in which economic restructuring is based on Knowledge driven Competition. Learning activities are widespread, and the welfare provisions remain	High flexibility of the work force without any social protection. Polarization and social exclusion at high level. No flexibility of the workforce and no social protection. High flexibility of the workforce in the framework of a strong social protection network. Polarization and social exclusion is minimized.

	the minimum safety net for innovation. Competition is based on the continuation of the existed structures and practices. Knowledge is not considered a driven factor. Context in which economic restructuring is based on the reduction of the welfare provisions and Knowledge and learning is not considered an important factor for competition.	Full time employment and strong social protection provisions.
Hungary	Stagnation Not trusting Traditional response Global interest	Immobility Traditional employee and modern organisation. Traditional organisation and modern employee. Modernisation of the organisation and employee.
Luxembourg/ Belgium	Stagnation Economic thinking Reactive approach Adaptive environment	Traditional organisational scheme Focus on organisation Focus on worker Interaction
Poland		Autarchy Colonial model Unmet readiness Full synergy
Slovenia	Rigidity Socially controlled modernisation Deepening of social inequalities Flexibility	Rigid, non-polarised labour market Rigid, polarised labour market Modernised and regulated labour market Liberal labour market
United Kingdom		

In the second phase, the countries refined their scenarios and brought down the number of scenarios to three. United Kingdom and Germany developed four scenarios and Poland two.

3.4. Contours of overarching scenarios at European level

In phase 1 European scenarios have been identified and discussed. However, they served as a point of reference for the further development of the national and European scenarios. An objective of phase 2 was therefore to develop three or four meta scenarios for VET going beyond the specific contexts on the European level as well as on the national levels. Contexts A and B from phase 1 were then merged. These overarching scenarios should be elaborated at both national and European levels and draw from medium and longer term perspectives.

Comparing the European components or scenario dimensions with the dimensions developed within the participating countries, we can see some similarities and some differences.

In the context of Economy and technology, one scenario dimension, that of economic restructuring, was commonly used. On the second scenario dimension how-ever there is difference of opinion. There are two scenario themes that came up in the analysis of several countries:
- Increasing ICT driven innovation and competition;
- Economic actors' responsibility and co-operation in VET.

In context B, employment and the labour market, there seem to be three dimensions that can be recognised across the countries and at the European level:
- Increasing flexibility and mobility of labour;
- Modernisation of the work place (and work organisation);
- Tackling social exclusion.

In the context of training, skills and knowledge the main themes of the scenario dimensions are more diverse. In the European analysis we came up with four dimensions. Comparison with the country analysis resulted also in four scenario dimensions, more or less differently formulated. These are:
- Individualisation;
- Partnerships and networks between public and private providers of training;
- Importance of non-formal training;

- Continuing and life long learning.

In the second phase/follow up of the project we combined the different dimensions that were developed across the contexts, to come up with a few meta-scenarios. We have done this in a way that the European dimensions were regarded as an 'overarching umbrella' that covers most of the dimensions developed at the national level. Such meta-or overarching scenarios were developed in the second phase and the focus as it has been said above was in this stage more on the question of strategies, linked with the scenarios developed so far which, however, were further re-fined and verified too.

Table 16: **Common elements put into reference-scenarios**

	LOW DEGREE OF MODERNISATION OF THE WORKPLACE	**HIGH DEGREE OF MODERNISATION OF THE WORKPLACE**
Weak economic restructuring for competitiveness	**1. Scenario The Cube** The system closed to globalisation, international co-operation and European integration. Internal stagnation both on the labour market and at the work place. Narrow competencies make mobility of labour force difficult. Low level of social and educational security. It is less important that partnerships in VET will be intensified. Technological Innovation will neither change social relationship employers and employees nor the structure of companies. New technology would not be very demanding to economic actors, they need not to take more responsibility in VET. Context in which organisa-	**2. Scenario The Elips** The system opened for globalisation processes but internally not prepared to cope with international competition. High degree of social security enabled by introducing imported systemic solutions but without mature internal conditions. 'Brain drain' of qualified labour force. The development of new ways of cooperation between employers is less important. Companies will have to restructure to remain competitive. Economic actors have far too many reasons to take over responsibilities of VET without being pressed by the needs of new technology. Context in which organisa-

tions stick to traditional patterns and personnel show no eagerness for innovation in their labour pattern.
Context in which little change is being integrated and personnel submitted to rigid working forms.

tions change their internal structure and processes and at the same time the labour force will not adopt these new practices.
Context in which the focus of change is on the company, whereas not enough efforts are made to make people follow.

Strong economic restructuring for competitiveness

3. Scenario The Circle

High degree of flexibility of labour force. Mutual adaptability of the labour and the work place. Enterprises develop their own internal training systems and flexible organisation structures. Neo-liberal solutions. Low level of social security and no support for lifelong learning activities for elderly people. Limited globalisation. The context possible in the case of lack of internal support for European integration or unmet readiness for integration on the side of the EU. To intensify partnership in VET will be important. To be competitive a change of structures in companies will not occur.
While new technology will necessitate many changes, economic actors may let the bulk of the responsibility of VET to other actors. Context in which individual workers are able and willing to work and live in new forms while at

4. Scenario The Fractal

Context in which there is a full synergy between internal and external factors deciding upon labour market development. Flexibilisation of labour force increases in accordance with the labour market needs and people's life style. Mutual adaptability of the labour market and the work place develops. Globalisation will help to increase social security though the economy can be affected by the 'brain drain'. Manyfold and intensified partnerships in VET will be more important. Due to technological innovation enterprises will restructure and social tensions will occur.
In a world experiencing the impact of new technology, economic actors should take more responsibility in facing the challenge in VET, too. Context in which there is a synergy between organisational and individual modernisation.

| the same time firms and companies show little innovation in their internal organisation. Context in which workers are willing to bring in and to follow new pathways, but in which the company structures remain traditional. | Context in which a high degree of interaction is created between the development of the company and the one of its personnel. |

The four scenarios formulated at a European level have their functions: they served as reference to the improvement, sharpening of the national scenarios.

3.5. Improved scenarios at national levels (2nd phase)

Dimensions

On the European level three dimensions were used:
- Economy and technology
- Employment and the labour market
- Training, skills and knowledge

In the training, skills and knowledge dimension only the demand site of training was to be taken into account. As mentioned in chapter 2, for each dimension several descriptors were distinguished. The countries wrote the scenarios according to these descriptors, but they used some of the descriptors, not all of them. Due to these differences in descriptor use, it was very hard to compare the scenarios. They differed too much. It was then decided that all countries had to use at least the four main descriptors:

Context A: restructuring, growth, competition, privatisation;
Context B: flexibility/mobility, work/training pattern, inequalities, organisation of labour;
Context C: general skills, in company training, willingness to invest, life long learning.

Table 17: **Main descriptors**

DIMENSIONS	MAIN DESCRIPTORS
Economy	Restructuring Growth Competition Privatisation
Social Labour dimension	Flexibility Work-training patterns Inequalities Organisation of labour
Training	General skills In-company training Willingness to invest Life long learning

To enhance the comparability, the countries were asked to quantify the descriptors, using a 5-point scale.
1 few/little/weak
2
3
4
5 many/much/strong

Example: take the descriptors growth, competition, inequalities and willingness to invest. It can be said that there's much or little growth, much or little competition, much or little willingness to invest and many or few inequalities in a certain scenario. The scores varied between 1 and 5. Table 18 contains the quantitative scores on the twelve descriptors. The countries are ranked alphabetically. In table 20 the scenarios are ranked by score.

Table 18: **Quantitative scores on the descriptors 1**

	RESTRUCTURING	GROWTH	COMPETITION	PRIVATISATION	FLEXIBILITY	WORK-TRAINING PATTERNS	INEQUALITIES	ORGANISATION OF LABOUR	GENERAL SKILLS	IN COMPANY TRAINING	WILLINGNESS TO INVEST	LIFE LONG LEARNING	AVERAGE
Austria, Internationalisation	5	4	5	5	5		5		3	3	5	5	4.5 (3.75)
Austria, Harmonisation	3-4	4		3	3-4		3		4-5	2	3	5	3.5 (2.6)
Austria, Regionalisation	3-4	3-4	3	2	2-3		1-2		5	4-5	3	5	3.4 (2.8)
Czech Republic, Scepticism to changes	2	1	2	2	3	3	3	3	3	2	3	2	2.4
Czech Republic, Growth solidarity	4	4	4	4	3	3	3	4	4	4	4	4	3.75
Czech Republic, Growth competitiveness	5	5	5	5	4	4	4	4	4	4	5	4	4.4
Estonia, Dissolving	4	5	5	4	5	4	4	4	5	4-5	4	5	4.5
Estonia, Good start	2	2-3	2-3	3	2	2	3	3	4	2	2	3	2.6

Estonia, Splitting into two	4	4	3-4	4	4	3	5	4	4-5	3	3-5	4	3.9
Germany, Context scenario A	4	4	3	4	5		5	2	4	4	4	4	3.9 (3.6)
Germany, Context scenario B	3	3	4	4	4		4	3	3	X	4	4	3.6 (3.0)
Germany, Context scenario C	4	4	3	3	4		4	3	4	X	4	4	3.7 (3.1)
Germany, Context scenario D	3	3	4	3	3		3	4	3	X	3	3	3.2 (2.7)
Greece, Competitive economy III	5	5	5	3	4	5	3	5	4	5	5	5	4.5
Greece, Individual and selective resp.	4	4	4	4	4	4	4	4	4	4	4	4	4
Greece, Complete domination of the market	5	3	5	5	5	3	5	3	5	2	3	3	3.9
Luxemb./Belgium, Controlled globalisation	5	4	3-4	5	5	4	5	2	3	4	4	5	4.1
Luxemb./Belgium, State regulation	5	5	3-4	5	5	5	3	5	2-3	5	4-5	5	4.5

Luxemb./ Belgium, Proximity of training	5	3	4-5	5	5	5	3	5	4-5	5	5	5	4.6
Poland, Limited development	3	3	4	3	2	3	4	3	3	3	2	4	3.1
Poland, Growth, co-operation and competition	5	4	3	5	4	4	3	4	5	4	4	5	4.2
Slovenia, Economic and social crisis	2	2	2	3	3-4	3	5	3	2-3	2	2		2.7 (2.5)
Slovenia, Slow and steady growth	4	4	3-4	3	3	4	3-4	4	3-4	3-4	3-4		3.6 (3.3)
Slovenia, Economic growth and flexibility	4-5	5	4-5	4-5	4-5	4-5	2-3	4	4-5	4-5	4		4.3 (3.9)
United Kingdom, Ad hoc responses to global pressures	3	2	2	3	3	2	3	2	3	2	2	2	2.4
United Kingdom, Crisis looms and the big players step in	5	1	1	1	2	2	3	2	3	2	2	2	2.2

United Kingdom, Free market approach to competitiveness	4	4	5	4	4	3	5	3	4	3	3	3	3.8
United Kingdom Social partnership approach	4	3	4	1	3	4	2	4	4	4	4	4	3.4

The actual averages of the scenarios vary between 2.2 (United Kingdom, crisis looms and the big players step in) and 4.6 (Luxembourg/Belgium, proximity of training). In some cases we didn't receive scores on all descriptors. Slovenia for ex-ample has no scores on the descriptor 'life long learning'. This made it harder to find the means. To get the mean, the sum of the scores was divided by 11, instead of by 12 (1 descriptor was missing). This is the score we used. Between the brackets the score was divided by 12, even though there's one descriptor less. Naturally this score is lower than the previous score. From Estonia we didn't receive enough scores to find the mean.

In table 19 we give a list of the revised and improved scenarios of the countries in phase 2.

Table 19: **Scenarios phase 2**

1a	Czech Republic	Scepticism to change (scenario I)
1b	Czech Republic	Growth-solidarity (scenario II)
1c	Czech Republic	Growth-competitiveness (scenario III)
2a	United Kingdom	Crisis looms and the big players step in (scenario I)
2b	United Kingdom	Ad hoc responses to global pressures (scenario II)
2c	United Kingdom	The free market approach to competitiveness on course (scenario III a)

2d	United Kingdom	A social partnership approach to competitiveness develops (scenario III b)
3a	Luxembourg/Belgium	Controlled globalisation (scenario I)
3b	Luxembourg/Belgium	Regulation (scenario II)
3c	Luxembourg/Belgium	Proximity of training (scenario III)
4a	Slovenia	Economic and social crisis (scenario I)
4b	Slovenia	Slow and steady (controlled) growth (scenario II)
4c	Slovenia	Economic growth and flexibility (scenario III)
5a	Estonia	Good start (scenario I)
5b	Estonia	Splitting into two (scenario II)
5c	Estonia	Dissolving (scenario III)
6a	Austria	Internationalisation (scenario I)
6b	Austria	Harmonization (scenario II)
6c	Austria	Regionalisation (scenario III)
7a	Greece	Complete domination of the market and increased inequalities on multiple levels (scenario I)
7b	Greece	Individual and selective responses to the effects of globalisation (scenario II)
7c	Greece	Competitive economy- lifelong learning- new dimensions in social policy (scenario III)
8a	Poland	Limited development/ad hoc adjustments (scenario I)
8b	Poland	Growth, Cooperation and competition (scenario II)
9a	Germany	Context scenario A
9b	Germany	Context scenario B
9c	Germany	Context scenario C
9d	Germany	Context scenario D

3.6. Clusters of scenarios at European level

The scenarios can be divided in three categories. Low scores, average scores and high scores.
- < 3.5
- 3.5 - 4.5
- ≥ 4.5

Below you can find a table with the scenarios ranked by average score. It starts with the scenario with the lowest score and ends with the scenario with the highest score.

Table 20: **Average scores per scenario**

COUNTRY	SCENARIO	AVERAGE
Low scores < 3.5		
United Kingdom	Crisis looms and big players step in	2.2
United Kingdom	Ad hoc responses to global pressures	2.4
Czech Republic	Scepticism to changes	2.4
Estonia	Good start	2.6
Slovenia	Economic and social crisis	2.7 (2.5)
Poland	Limited development	3.1
Germany	Context scenario D	3.2
Austria	Regionalisation	3.4 (2.8)
United Kingdom	Social partnership approach	3.4
Average scores 3.5 - 4.5		
Austria	Harmonisation	3.5 (2.6)
Slovenia	Slow and steady growth	3.6 (3.3)
Germany	Context scenario B	3.6 (3.0)
Germany	Context scenario C	3.7 (3.1)
Czech Republic	Growth solidarity	3.8
United Kingdom	Free market approach still on course	3.8

Estonia	Splitting into two	3.9
Germany	Context scenario A	3.9 (3.6)
Greece	Complete domination of market	3.9
Greece	Individual and selective responses	4.0
Luxembourg/Belgium	Controlled globalisation	4.1
Poland	Growth, cooperation and competition	4.2
Slovenia	Economic growth and flexibility	4.3 (3.9)
Czech Republic	Growth competitiveness	4.4
High scores ≥ 4.5		
Estonia	Dissolving	4.5
Austria	Internationalisation	4.5 (3.75)
Luxembourg/Belgium	State regulation	4.5
Greece	Competitive economy - III	4.5
Luxembourg/Belgium	Proximity of training	4.6

The middle category contains the biggest part of the scenarios. Most countries have scenarios of quite different content for each of the three categories. Only Greece, Luxembourg/Belgium, Slovenia and United Kingdom have two scenarios in the same category.

United Kingdom has low averages in general. Three of the four scenarios are listed in the category 'low scores'. Conversely Luxembourg/Belgium has fairly high scores. Two of their scenarios are included in the category 'high scores'.

The averages of the scenarios can also be ranked per dimension. Within each dimension the scores are compared and put in order, starting with the lowest score.

Table 21: **Averages per dimension**

COUNTRY	SCENARIO	AVERAGE
Economy		
Czech Republic	Scepticism to changes	1.75
Slovenia	Economic and social crisis	2.25
United Kingdom	Crisis looms and the big players step in	2.25
United Kingdom	Ad hoc responses to global pressures	2.50
Estonia	Good start	2.50
United Kingdom	Social partnership approach	3.00
Austria	Regionalisation	3.00
Poland	Limited development	3.25
Germany	Context scenario D	3.25
Austria	Harmonization	3.50 (2.63)
Germany	Context scenario B	3.50
Germany	Context scenario C	3.50
Slovenia	Slow and steady growth	3.63
Germany	Context scenario A	3.75
Estonia	Splitting into two	3.88
Greece	Individual and selective responses	4.00
Czech Republic	Growth solidarity	4.00
United Kingdom	Free market approach to competitiveness	4.25
Luxembourg/Belgium	Controlled globalisation	4.38
Luxembourg/Belgium	Proximity of training	4.38
Estonia	Dissolving	4.50
Greece	Complete domination of market	4.50
Greece	Competitive economy -III-	4.50
Luxembourg/Belgium	State regulation	4.63
Slovenia	Economic growth and flex	4.63

Austria	Internationalisation	4.75
Poland	Growth, coop. And comp.	4.75
Czech Republic	Growth competitiveness	5.00

Social labour

Austria	Regionalisation	2.00 (1.00)
United Kingdom	Crisis looms and the big players step in	2.25
United Kingdom	Ad hoc responses to global pressures	2.50
Estonia	Good start	2.50
Czech Republic	Scepticism to changes	3.00
Czech Republic	Growth solidarity	3.25
United Kingdom	Social partnership approach	3.25
Austria	Harmonization	3.25 (1.63)
Germany	Context scenario D	3.33 (2.5)
Slovenia	Economic and social crisis	3.63
Slovenia	Slow and steady growth	3.63
Germany	Context scenario B	3.67 (2.75)
Germany	Context scenario C	3.67 (2.75)
United Kingdom	Free market approach to competitiveness	3.75
Poland	Growth, coop. and comp.	3.75
Slovenia	Economic growth and flex	3.88
Germany	Context scenario A	4.00 (3.00)
Estonia	Splitting into two	4.00
Czech Republic	Growth competitiveness	4.00
Poland	Limited development	4.00
Luxembourg/Belgium	Controlled globalisation	4.00
Greece	Individual and selective responses	4.00
Greece	Complete domination of market	4.00
Greece	Competitive economy -III	4.25

Estonia	Dissolving	4.25
Luxembourg/Belgium	State regulation	4.50
Luxembourg/Belgium	Proximity of training	4.50
Austria	Internationalisation	5.00 (2.50)
Training		
Slovenia	Economic and social crisis	2.20 (1.62)
United Kingdom	Ad hoc responses to global pressures	2.25
United Kingdom	Crisis looms and the big players step in	2.25
Czech Republic	Scepticism to changes	2.50
Estonia	Good start	2.75
Poland	Limited development	3.00
Germany	Context scenario D	3.00 (2.25)
United Kingdom	Free market approach to competitiveness	3.25
Greece	Complete domination of market	3.25
Slovenia	Slow and steady growth	3.50 (2.63)
Austria	Harmonization	3.63
Germany	Context scenario B	3.67 (2.75)
Estonia	Splitting into two	3.75
Germany	Context scenario C	4.00 (3.00)
Germany	Context scenario A	4.00
Austria	Internationalisation	4.00
Czech Republic	Growth solidarity	4.00
Greece	Individual and selective responses	4.00
United Kingdom	Social partnership approach	4.00
Luxembourg/Belgium	Controlled globalisation	4.00
Luxembourg/Belgium	State regulation	4.25
Czech Republic	Growth competitiveness	4.25
Slovenia	Economic growth and flex	4.33 (3.25)

Austria	Regionalisation	4.38
Poland	Growth, coop. and comp.	4.50
Estonia	Dissolving	4.62
Greece	Competitive economy - III	4.75
Luxembourg/Belgium	Proximity of training	4.88

The closer the scores are to each other, the less the scenarios differ on that dimension. Scores that are far apart belong to very different scenarios. For example on the training dimension: Luxembourg/Belgium (Proximity of training) and Slovenia (Economic and social crisis) really differ. The first has relatively high scores, the latter much lower scores. This implies that when clustering the scenarios these two will not be in the same cluster.

We clustered the scenarios on a theoretical basis, by placing the scores of the 27 scenarios on the economic and social dimensions in a graph. This resulted in 4 clusters. You can find the graph below (see figure 6).

This way of clustering divides the graph in 4 equal quadrants, thus creating 4 clusters of scenarios. We present two alternatives in figure 6. The first is based on a 2.5 position line and the other on a 3.5 position line. As can be seen, a clustering like this leads to an uneven distribution of scenarios. Most scenarios in this first alternative can be found in the quadrant with a high score on the economy dimension and a high score on the labour dimension. In theory all the quadrants are possible, but in practice it appears that the upper right quadrant is clearly more popular than the others. In the second variant we see a division of especially the second quadrant.

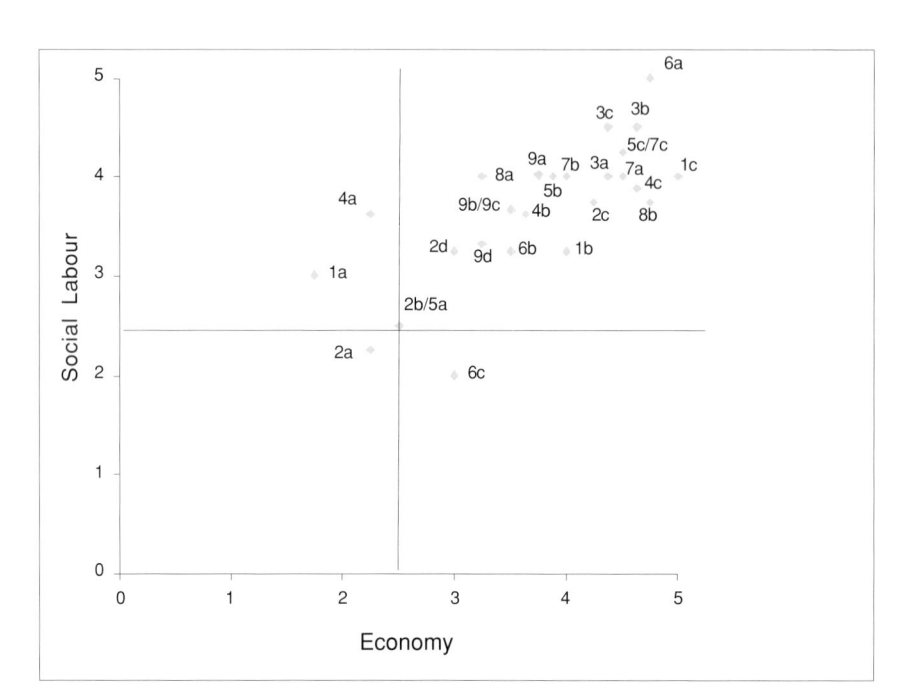

Figure 6: **Scenario scores on the economic and labour dimension**

The four scenarios are labelled as follows:
- Europe and education: always ahead. This a scenario in which the economic development is piping the tune, social aspects are following this development with a certain distance. Economic restructuring is a prime mover in society.
- Europe and education: rising high. This is a scenario in which Europe develops itself widely in both economic and socials spheres. The economic and social domains are encouraging each other and create a synergic effect.
- Europe and education: still together. This is a scenario in which there is down-ward development in Europe. Maybe not a crisis but certainly not a road ahead. Economic and social aspects are nevertheless in pace with each other although at a low level of development.
- Europe and education: it's worth it. This is a scenario in which the economic development is lagging behind the social infrastructure. Although the economic development might be at a relatively low level the general feeling in Europe is that aspect as social inclusion, migration and integration do re-quire that social emphasis.

In the project we used 12 descriptors to work out the four scenarios. If we apply these descriptors to 4 scenarios in the last clustering we can give an overview as follows.

Table 22: **Europe and education: always ahead**

	EUROPE AND EDUCATION: ALWAYS AHEAD
Economic restructuring	There is a constant economic restructuring, open to the rigours of global competition.
Economic growth	Economic growth is at a high level, growth is sustained in the market driven economy.
Economic competition	Economic competition is fierce.
Economic privatisation	Most state companies are in a process of complete or partial privatisation.
Social flexibility	People do organize their work in a flexible way.
Social work-training patterns	There is certain pressure from the private sector on the state to perform a more active role in the field of training; individualization is not in line with the economic needs.
Social inequalities	High turn over rate of jobs accelerate social differentiations.
Social organization of labour	Majority of companies adapt new patterns like teamwork, job sharing, quality control, just-in-time production.
Training demand for general skills	General skills needed because of the overall and rapid economic restructuring, businesses have too much relied on a low skills equilibrium.
Training demand for in company training	In-firm training and private provision is important.
Training demand and willingness to invest	Companies are very willing to invest in training.
Training demand for life long learning	LLL is an important aspect of this scenario. Employability is a main impetus for LLL. Partnerships are partially developed.

Table 23: **Europe and education: rising high**

	EUROPE AND EDUCATION: RISING HIGH
Economic restructuring	Economic restructuring is a main feature of Europe's development.
Economic growth	Growth is to be seen in all economic sectors.
Economic competition	Governments intervene little, leaving the entrepreneur free.
Economic privatisation	Privatisation is tempered; the public sector is regaining some of its importance.
Social flexibility	Individualization of work arrangements is prevailing.
Social work-training patterns	Individual differences regarding learning and lifestyles are valued to high degree, some companies operate as learning organizations.
Social inequalities	Partnerships promote equity and opportunity.
Social organization of labour	Companies adapt quickly to reorganizations, flatter hierarchies are prevailing, SME's are popular forms of work.
Training demand for general skills	New transferable skills and competencies ought to be integrated into the curricula.
Training demand for in company training	Dual learning schemes are modernized and popular.
Training demand and willingness to invest	Both firms and individuals are investors in training.
Training demand for life long learning	LLL is important: its motives are both economically (employability) and socially (especially individual arrangement between work, care and learning periods). Strategies are coherently developed with full partnership.

Table 24: **Europe and education: still together**

	EUROPE AND EDUCATION: STILL TOGETHER
Economic restructuring	There is no general tendency. Restructuring is restricted to certain companies and certain sectors of the economy.
Economic growth	National instability as part of a wider global cycle; faltering economy.
Economic competition	Partnership spot economic and social signals but it is all at a low level.
Economic privatisation	Privatisation is incrementally adopted and executed in slow process.
Social flexibility	Flexibility is not a characteristic, but on the other hand there isn't too much need for it.
Social work-training patterns	The relationship between skills needs and supply remains ad hoc. Neither planning nor market was successful in filling certain gaps.
Social inequalities	Debate on the acceptance of a substantial degree of inequality in the process of rebalancing the economy and fostering economic growth.
Social organization of labour	Traditional patterns prevail as companies and the state are uncertain how to react to mondialization.
Training demand for general skills	Formal qualifications are in line with the overall social economic situation, there isn't much demand for new skills.
Training demand for in company training	In-company training is part of the traditional training schemes, more modern forms are not developed.
Training demand and willingness to invest	Investment in LLL is on a relatively low level.
Training demand for life long learning	LLL is only in certain areas of the economy a prevailing aspect, it is not something of society as a whole. Demand is low and there is no coherent development.

Table 25: **Europe and education: it's worth it**

	EUROPE AND EDUCATION: IT'S WORTH IT
Economic restructuring	There is a slow down of Europe's development. Economic restructuring is certainly not a main issue.
Economic growth	Economy is stagnating, manufacturing and agriculture are in decline.
Economic competition	Europe is loosing its competitive edge, productivity is declining, inward investment is evaporating vastly.
Economic privatisation	The public sector is seen as a means of mass employment and privatisation has stopped.
Social flexibility	There is not much flexibility although it would certainly be needed.
Social work-training patterns	Identifying and meeting skills need is an important part of the government-led partnership process.
Social inequalities	Social exclusion has to be combated. That is prevailing characteristic. It is worth very much because the social structure of Europe depends on it.
Social organization of labour	Companies might need to reduce the size of the workforce and strengthen the hierarchical structure.
Training demand for general skills	In the economic sphere only some specific sectors do ask for new general skills. The social domain is renewed and new skills are asked for, however the economic basis of it is thin and sometimes absent.
Training demand for in company training	The state is encouraging training programmes, only a few companies continue to offer high quality training.
Training demand and willingness to invest	Investment is mainly encouraged by public social programmes subsidized by the state.
Training demand for life long learning	LLL is seen mainly as an instrument for disadvantaged groups. It belongs especially to the social domain.

The 4 clusters of scenarios can be placed in figure 6 (see chapter 5.6), which results in the graph presented below (figure 7). It shows where the scenarios are situated on the economic and social dimension.

Figure 7 represents the position of the scenarios in the four quadrants in diagram form.

Figure 7: **Clusters of scenarios**

SOCIAL LABOUR	**ECONOMY**	**ECONOMY DIMENSION**
Social labour dimension	Europe and education: it's worth it	Europe and education: rising high
	Europe and education: still together	Europe and education: always ahead

The second quadrant, Europe and education: rising high has a high score on the economic and social labour dimension, while the third quadrant Europe and education: still together scores low on both dimensions.

Europe and education: always ahead scores high on economy, but the social developments are lagging behind. Europe and education: rising high and Europe and education: still together are balanced scenarios. The first scenario has a high score on both the economic and the social dimension, the latter has a low score on both dimensions. Europe and education: it's worth it, has a low economic development, but invests a lot in social matters. Even if the economic situation doesn't allow it.

3.7. Questionnaire on EU-level

The final step in the project, is a questionnaire sent to experts working on the EU-level. Cedefop and ETF wanted to involve some actors and stakeholders working on the European level, e.g. in the European Commission and other EU-institutions and in EU-level social partner organizations, Committees and advisory bodies, to find out whether they could work with this addition to their working repertoire: combining strategies and scenarios in debating the future of vocational education.

The questionnaire consists of three parts. In the first part, questions are asked concerning the (categories of) strategies. What is done at the European level with regard to certain strategies and what else could be done? In the second part the three clusters of scenarios are presented and the experts were asked to add aspects to these clusters in order to enhance their relevance for European level debates. The third part is about the robustness of strategies in relation to their frequency. What can be said about the discrepancies in relevance/frequency and robustness? The results of the analysis can be found in chapter 6.

3.8. Links with recent EU scenario developments

The European Commission's Forward Studies Unit developed in 1999 scenarios on overall European policy development. On the basis of five major topics chosen as the starting point of their work:
- Development of institutions and governance;
- Social cohesion;
- Economic adaptability;
- Enlargement of the EU; and
- The international context

This group bundled a number of variables relating to potential scenarios, allocated them to various players and then interviewed high-ranking decision-makers from the Commission and other EU institutions, brought them together in workshops and worked out alternatives with them. Finally they arrived at five scenarios, which they termed 'coherent, concerted and plausible images', representing the spectrum of possibilities, factors and players which could in future play a crucial role.
- Scenario 1, The Triumph of the Market, is characterised, as its name implies, by the absolute dominance of economic liberalism and the free exchange of goods and services. Europe, whatever its standard, would hardly be different from the rest of the world, which would then be a single planetary market.
- Scenario 2, A Hundred Flowers, is typified by growing paralysis (and corruption) of major public and private institutions. Europeans withdraw to the lo-cal and micro level and to a primarily informal economy entailing a duplication of initiatives with no logical connection.

- Scenario 3, Divided Responsibilities, is based on the hypothesis of metamorphosis of the public sector against a background of positive economic development, which could engender renewed social and industrial policies.
- Scenario 4, The Developing Society, depicts a society undergoing extensive transformation in respect of socio-economic and political developments under the premise that this time ecological and human development values prevail. It includes a basically workable new form of humanism and paves the way for an 'immaterial and global renaissance'.
- Scenario 5, The Turbulent Neighbourhood, depicts a weakened Europe in con-junction with sudden and deeply disturbed geopolitical developments, both in the East and in the South, with growing tensions and conflicts causing a 'European Security Council' to be entirely concerned with questions of de-fence and security.

These scenarios reveal one thing: they show that the search for a vision for Europe, its institutions, its identity and geopolitical stabilisation is still in full swing. The process of enlargement is not yet complete, and the broad-based consensus to find the socio-economic direction which Europe could take in the next 10 years is still relatively open. The further stabilisation of Europe with a maximum guarantee of economic and social prosperity can, at present, be regarded as a doubtful hypothesis.

If we compare the two sets of scenarios (table 26), we can see a certain overlap between them. In some cases two of our scenarios match one European scenario.

Table 26: **European Commission scenarios and the scenarios in this project compared**

EUROPEAN SCENARIOS	SCENARIOS OF THIS PROJECT
Triumph of the market	Europe and education: always ahead
Divided responsibility	Europe and education: it's worth it / rising high
A hundred flowers	Europe and education: still together
The developing society	Europe and education: rising high/ it's worth it
The turbulent neighbourhood	Europe and education: still together

4. Development of strategies

4.1. Strategy development in phase 1

In this chapter we will discuss the development of the strategies in the first phase and their clustering in the three contexts. Then we will present the strategy clustering's that were done by the countries. The different clusters were hard to compare, so it was decided to cluster the strategies also on European level. This is done in paragraph 6.2.

In phase 1 we explored for the European analysis several techniques in order to get a clustering of the strategies. To reach our goal, exploring the data in a tentative way, we decided finally to treat the 'not relevant' question, which is a dichotomous variable, as a semi-interval variable. Although this is not a fully justified technique with this data, we can do this because there is only one interval in dichotomous variables, so the condition of equal intervals is always fulfilled (De Heus et al, 1995, pp 37). This analysis resulted in the following strategies:

Strategies in context A

SA1   A strategy based on providing incentives for the private sector and social partners to engage in training (s07 s16 s17 s20)

This strategy clusters the elements in which the involvement of the private sector and social partners is stimulated to develop education and training in new technology, in exchange programs across Europe and to achieve widespread recognition for the value of VET certificates.

SA2   A strategy based on forecasting specific needs (s09 s10 s14 s19)

This strategy is composed of actions that ensure that specific training is provided in response to changing practices, like the need for non-technical, social elements in technical training courses and new combinations of training and employment, by forecasting future economic trends.

SA3   A strategy based on the learning organisation and knowledge management (s06 s12 s13 s18)

This strategy is especially directed towards the role of knowledge within the lives of individuals, preparing them for 'life-long-learning', promoting acquiring knowledge of employees within firms, but also ensuring that firms themselves become learning organisations.

Strategies in context B

SB1   A strategy based on the modern worker: flexible, part time, employable, entrepreneurial (s04 s05 s10 s11)

The elements clustered in this strategy describe a variety of actions promoting flexibility, mobility, employability, but also the teaching and learning of entrepreneurial skills.

SB2   A strategy based on supporting structures(s12 s17 s18 s19)

This strategy describes actions concerned with supporting structures, like employ-ment agencies focusing on the provision of counselling and support for training, in addition to their traditional intermediary role. But also providing support in general like developing a social security policy that subsidises labour costs, providing training for all young people to attain a basic level of technical training, and better systems of support for the well-being of employees.

SB3   A strategy based on target groups especially groups at risk (s01 s02 s03 s06)

This strategy combines actions directed at providing work, training and guidance for disadvantaged people on the job market and within firms, facilitating ways for people to alternate between periods of work, training and caring.

Strategies in context C

SC1   A strategy based on a transparent qualification structure and mobility (s12 s15 s17 s18)

This strategy clusters actions that will harmonise and align qualifications and make them flexible within the VET system, but also between different countries. Related to this are actions that will enable people to be mobile and flexible in the ways they acquire qualifications.

SC2   A strategy based on personal development against social exclusion (s02 s06 s07 s09)

The elements that are clustered in this strategy are all related to taking action by providing vocational education and training and flexible programmes of work, training, guidance and guidance for people from certain disadvantaged groups that will equip them with a solid basis for their further personal development. In general this strategy emphasizes the important role of training in achieving (or maintaining) social solidarity, and in combating social divisions and social exclusion.

SC3   A strategy based on specific basic skills (s13 s14)

This strategy is composed of actions directed at promoting and developing the need for successive, serial specialisations like handling and/or managing information, because specialisation in one skill enables the acquisition of further skills in time, which is the most important skill in vocational education and training.

 SC4 A strategy based on age-specific groups (s08 s11 s19)

The fourth strategy in context C clusters actions that need to be taken for young and especially older people to provide better vocational education and training opportunities and more guidance concerning career choices. Also firms should be stimulated to integrate training with their human resource and planning systems.

 SC5 A strategy based on individuals investing in their own training (s01 s10)

This strategy is directed towards motivating individuals to invest more in their own training and development, for example by financing training to a larger degree by providing individuals with tax incentives.

Table 27: **Clusters of strategies in the contexts**

CONTEXT	EUROPEAN LEVEL
Context A	A strategy based on providing incentives for the private sector and social partners to engage in training. A strategy based on forecasting specific needs A strategy based on the learning organisation and knowledge management.
Context B	A strategy based on the modern worker: flexible, part time, employ-able, entrepreneurial A strategy based on supporting structures A strategy based on target groups especially groups at risk
Context C	A strategy based on a transparent qualification structure and Mobility A strategy based on personal development against social exclusion A strategy based on specific basic skills A strategy based on age-specific groups A strategy based on individuals investing in their own training

4.2. Further development of strategies (phase 2)

Earlier we explained how scenarios can be explicitly incorporated in the process of formulating strategies. With that it is fairly essential to grasp the difference between a strategy and a scenario. Scenarios describe possible trends, whereas strategies pre-sent options for action in response to these potential developments. Scenarios provide a testing-ground for strategies or, to put it another way, they are the wind-tunnels in which different strategic options can be tested out. The aim is to work out the various possible strategies within the different scenarios (Van der Heijden 1996).

Strategies indicate ways of dealing with the different futures. Scenario planning is therefore both an autonomous and a strategic activity. Autonomous, in the sense that the focus is on possible variations of factors that cannot be influenced directly (scenarios). It is also a strategic activity, in the sense that the focus is on various possibilities of intervening in and influencing the course of events (strategies)

Every possible strategy can be translated into every scenario. The extent to which scenario and strategy are treated in an integrated fashion may vary. A strategy that only works well in one of the scenarios and in none of the others is certainly hazardous. We should therefore strive towards finding strategies that are robust in the sense that they have a purpose in several alternative futures.

Aggregated strategies
Each of the partner institutes grouped their strategies into clusters. The following clusters of strategies are constructed by the countries:

Austria
- Strengthening of private offerings
- Development of prognosis instruments
- Learning organisations and knowledge management
- State preventative measures
- Age specific education and continuing education
- Modularisation of education and continuing education

Czech Republic
- Modern worker
- Incentive private sector
- Supporting structures

Estonia
- Developing a new VET infrastructure supplying all parties with information
- Pathways to education and labour market
- Flexible, mobile and life long learning employees

Germany
- Support for the private sector
- Accurate information
- Learning in the 'lives' of individuals, firms and communities
- Modern worker

Luxemburg/Belgium
- Networks within training systems
- Growth of responsibilities of companies in traing policies
- Training as part if the social policy
- Growth of flexiblity in the training system

United Kingdom
- Information
- Modernization
- Protection
- Social development

These clusters of strategies at national level aren't very comparable. In order to reach a comparable point of view we regrouped the strategies in certain categories. We based these categories on a mixed state/market model. We called that the model of market coordination by government and distinguished four categories of strategies.

In order to cluster the strategies on European level, 4 x 2 categories were developed with regard to the clusters made by the project teams. The clusters are based on a model called market coordination by government in which the government plays a determining role in the coordination of the market. Demand and supply must be in proportion in this market situation. Therefore information is a necessary condition. A market can't exist by itself, it must be created and the government should act as market supervisor. The clusters based on this market coordination model are listed below.

I Demand
   1   Modern worker strategy
   2   Individual is financially responsible for own training strategy

II Supply
   1   Flexible providers/networks of providers strategy
   2   More training within firms/learning organizations strategy

III Information
   1   Forecasting strategy
   2   Transparency/availability strategy

IV Coordination (market coordination by governments)
   1   Monitoring (quality control, free entrance of new providers, counter monopolies) strategy
   2   Protection strategy

The country strategies are classified in the clusters mentioned above. In each category all countries are listed with the strategies that fit in the category. Often, the country strategies aren't equally divided over the categories. There can be several strategies in one category or even no strategies at all. It depends on what's considered important by a country. Each country was free to work out it's own accents.

As you will see, some categories are more 'popular' than others. Cluster IV.1 (co-ordination; monitoring) for example contains only three strategies, while 26 strategies are placed in cluster I.1 (demand; modern worker) and IV.2 (coordination; protection). It's possible that certain clusters are more important than others, but it's also possible that the countries didn't take into consideration every aspect. The skewness of the popularity of strategies gives an insight in what might be missing as far as strategies concerned.

I Demand
   1   Modern worker strategy

European strategies
   B1:   A strategy based on the modern worker: flexible, part time, employable, entrepreneurial
   C3:   A strategy based on specific basic skills

Austria
B1: Modern employees: encouragement of flexible, entrepreneurial thinking, mobile and self-responsible employees
B3: Life-long learning for all: establishment of the concept of 'life-long learning' within the labour force, employers and the creation of corresponding framework conditions for its transfer (for ex. movement between phases of employment and education and continuing education), especially also for 'risk' groups and discriminated persons
C2: Education and personality development: that tasks and roles of education and continuing education for the development of personality are recognised and encouraged

Czech Republic
B1: A strategy based on the modern worker: flexible, part time, employable, entrepreneurial
C3: A strategy based on specific basic skills

Estonia
B1: A strategy based on the modern worker: flexible, part time, employable, entrepreneurial
C3: A strategy based on specific basic skills

Germany
S4: Encourage the development of the 'modern' worker
S8: Concentrate on basic skills development
S11: Provide incentives for non-qualification based training
S13: Develop and implement life/work friendly policies

Greece
B1: A strategy based on the modern worker: flexible, part time, employable, entrepreneurial
C3: A strategy based on specific basic skills

Luxembourg/Belgium
B4: A strategy to provide training for job seekers adapted to the needs of the labour market
C3: A strategy to provide career guidance at different moments for all people

Poland
- B2: Strategy based on developing a new model of an employee: employable, flexible and enterprising
- C3: Strategy based on an intensive use of information techniques and on development of communication skills (Internet, foreign languages, etc.)
- C4: Strategy based on the development of interpersonal skills and self-instruction habits
- C7: Strategy based on the development of those educational areas that give the opportunity to compete in the EC labour market

Slovenia
Modernisation of VET content
Promotion of the key skills and social solidarity

United Kingdom
- S4: Encourage the development of the 'modern' worker
- S8: Concentrate on basic skills development
- S11: Provide incentives for non-qualification based training
- S13: Develop and implement life/work friendly policies

2 *Individual is financially responsible for own training strategy*

European
- C5: A strategy based on individuals investing in their own training

Austria
- C5: Individual responsibility: encouragement of individual education responsibility and education investment

Czech Republic
- C5: A strategy based on individuals investing in their own training

Estonia
- C5: A strategy based on individuals investing in their own training

Germany
- S3: Raise the profile of learning in the lives of individuals, in communities, in businesses
- S9: Encourage individuals to invest in their own training

Greece
C5: A strategy based on individuals investing in their own training

Luxembourg/Belgium

Poland
C6: Strategy based on an increased participation of individuals in financing the education

Slovenia
Promoting greater individual responsibility for its own education and training

United Kingdom
S3: Raise the profile of learning in the lives of individuals, in communities, in businesses
S9: Encourage individuals to invest in their own training

II Supply
1 *Flexible providers/networks of providers strategy*

European

Austria
A1: Strengthening of private offerings: encouraging the engagement of private offerings in the field of education/continuing education in rapidly developing fields, in coordination with the social partners
C1: Modularisation of education and continuing education: modularisation of education and continuing education with simultaneous widespread recognition of various types of achieved qualifications and diplomas
C4: Age specific education and continuing education: encouragement of life-long learning, especially through age specific education and continuing education offers

Czech Republic

Estonia

Germany
S12: Make optimal use of information technologies in training

Greece

Luxembourg/Belgium
A1: A strategy based on the establishment of physical and social networks between all actors involved in training
B2: A strategy to create more flexibility between the training and labour system
B3: A strategy to set up training networks
C1: A strategy to provide a competency-based and flexible system of alternance between training and working periods
C2: A strategy to develop training systems which are coherent between countries, between the different qualification levels and the various company strategies
C4: A strategy to create more flexible training opportunities

Poland
A3: Anticipation of the labour market needs, appropriate modification of vocational training profiles, and application of alternating forms of working periods and training
C1: Strategy based on an increased flexibility and diversification of education programmes

Slovenia
— Social arrangements for supporting greater flexibility and mobility of the labour force
— Promoting modular certification system and coherent, transparent qualification framework
Promoting education adapted to the personal needs

United Kingdom
S12: Make optimal use of information technologies in training

2 More training within firms/learning organizations strategy

European
A1: A strategy based on providing incentives for the private sector and social partners to engage in training.

A3: A strategy based on the learning organisation and knowledge management.

Austria
A3: Learning organisations and knowledge management: knowledge encouragement concerning, understanding of learning organisations and knowledge management with the goal of a comprehensive introduction/institutionalisation

Czech Republic
A1: A strategy based on providing incentives for the private sector and social partners to engage in training.
A3: A strategy based on the learning organisation and knowledge management.

Estonia
A1: A strategy based on providing incentives for the private sector and social partners to engage in training.
A3: A strategy based on the learning organisation and knowledge management.
Career counselling, linking training to enterprises' business plans

Germany
S1: Provide incentives for the private sector and social partners to engage in training
S10: Shift government funding from the demand side (employees/learners) to the supply side (trainers)

Greece
A1: A strategy based on providing incentives for the private sector and social partners to engage in training.
A3: A strategy based on the learning organisation and knowledge management

Luxembourg/Belgium
A2: A strategy based on strengthening the role of companies to engage in training

Poland
A1: Establishment of the systems of incentives for enterprises in order to make them invest in vocational education and training
A2: Involvement of social partners and, in particular, employers' and employees' organizations in the actions related to vocational education and training development
A4: Strategy based on the concept of 'learning organizations' and 'knowledge management'
B3: Establishment of local/regional networks connecting the vocational education and training organizers with entrepreneurs in order to ensure an appropriate supply of workers in local/regional labour markets
B4: Involvement of enterprises in the cooperation with organizers in the field of vocational education and training on preparing in-company training programmes
C9: Strategy based on a more active participation of companies in the process of education

Slovenia
— Greater role of companies in VET
— Greater investment of private sector in a life long learning

United Kingdom
S1: Provide incentives for the private sector and social partners to engage in training
S10: Shift government funding from the demand side (employees/learners) to the supply side (trainers)

III **Information**
1 Forecasting strategy

European
A2: A strategy based on forecasting specific needs

Austria
A2: Development of prognosis instruments: development of prognosis instruments, that quickly show developments and allow direct (so called just-in-time) reactions of the educational system to changed requirements

C3: Knowledge management: establishing knowledge management as a basic prerequisite for work and life

Czech Republic
A2: A strategy based on forecasting specific needs

Estonia
A2: A strategy based on forecasting specific needs

Germany

Greece
A2: A strategy based on forecasting specific needs

Luxembourg/Belgium
A3: A strategy based on the capacity to forecast specific training needs

Poland

Slovenia
— Developing mechanisms for forecasting and certification

United Kingdom

  3 *Transparency/availability strategy*

European
C1: A strategy based on a transparent qualification structure and mobility

Austria

Czech Republic
C1: A strategy based on a transparent qualification structure and mobility

Estonia
C1: A strategy based on a transparent qualification structure and mobility

Germany
S2: Produce accurate, up-to-date information about changing skills needs
S7: Produce a transparent qualification structure

Greece
C1: A strategy based on a transparent qualification structure and mobility

Luxembourg/Belgium

Poland
C8: Strategy based on a transparent classification of vocations and specialities and clear principles of professional promotion - comparable to EC

Slovenia

United Kingdom
S2: Produce accurate, up-to-date information about changing skills needs
S7: Produce a transparent qualification structure

IV **Coordination**
1 *Monitoring (quality control, new entrants, no monopolies) strategy*

European

Austria

Czech Republic

Estonia

Germany

Greece

Luxembourg/Belgium

Poland
C2: Strategy based on continuing education and retraining of employees
C10: Strategy based on increasing the number of workplaces and an eased entry of baby-boomers into the labour market

Slovenia
— Flexibilisation and deregulation of the local/regional labour markets 4.1

United Kingdom

2 Protection strategy

European
B2: A strategy based on supporting structures
B3: A strategy based on target groups especially groups at risk
C2: A strategy based on personal development against social exclusion
C4: A strategy based on age-specific groups

Austria
B2: State preventative measures: creation of state preventative measures, that secure the well-being of workers (health care, social contributions, etc)

Czech Republic
B2: A strategy based on supporting structures
B3: A strategy based on target groups especially groups at risk
C2: A strategy based on personal development against social exclusion
C4: A strategy based on age-specific groups

Estonia
B2: A strategy based on supporting structures
B3: A strategy based on target groups especially groups at risk
C2: A strategy based on personal development against social exclusion
C4: A strategy based on age-specific groups

Germany
S5: Develop information, guidance and support structures for individuals
S6: Target specific groups of people

Greece
B2: A strategy based on supporting structures
B3: A strategy based on target groups especially groups at risk
C2: A strategy based on personal development against social exclusion
C4: A strategy based on age-specific groups.

Luxembourg/Belgium
B1: A strategy to ensure that both public and private institutions provide not only training but also a larger social coverage.

Poland
B1: Integration of actions aimed at creating workplaces, as well as vocational training and guidance in order to increase the labour market opportunities of the disadvantaged groups of people.
C5: Strategy based on the education development aimed at combating social ex-clusion (unemployment, pathologies etc.).

Slovenia
— Promoting partnership in VET and life long learning for well being of em-ployees.
— Giving priority to VET for greater flexibility, mobility, and integration of disadvantaged groups.

United Kingdom
S5: Develop information, guidance and support structures for individuals.
S6: Target specific groups of people.

After the subdivision of the strategies it appeared that the strategies of most countries are spread over 6 of the 8 clusters. Poland and Slovenia have strategies in 7 clusters and Luxembourg/Belgium in 5. The strategies aren't divided equally over the clusters. Luxembourg/Belgium for example has a large concentration of strategies in cluster II.1 (supply: flexible providers/networks of providers) and hardly any strategies in the other clusters. This can be seen in table 28

Table 28: **Number of strategies per country in the clusters**

COUNTRY CLUSTER	EU	A	CZ	EE	D	EL	L/B	PL	SI	UK	TOTAL
Modern worker strategy	2	3	2	2	4	2	2	4	2	4	26
Individual is financially responsible strategy	1	1	1	1	2	1	-	1	1	2	11
Flexible (networks of) providers strategy	-	3	-	-	1	-	6	2	3	1	16
More training within firms	2	1	2	3	2	2	1	6	2	2	22
Forecasting	1	2	1	1	-	1	1	-	1	-	8
Transparency/ availability	1	-	1	1	2	1	-	1	-	2	9
Monitoring	-	-	-	-	-	-	-	2	1	-	3
Protection	4	1	4	4	2	4	1	2	2	2	26
Total	11	11	11	12	13	11	11	18	12	13	121

Table 28 shows the number of strategies per cluster and the number of strategies per country. Poland developed most strategies, 18 in total, 5 above average. Cluster I.1 (the modern worker strategy) and IV.2 (the protection strategy), the most popular clusters, contain 26 strategies, while cluster IV.1 (the monitoring strategy) is almost empty, it contains only three strategies.

4.3. Comparing recent EU policy strategies with the strategies developed in this project

In this paragraph we will present a table comparing the strategies as developed in this project with the strategies as formulated in recent EU Council Meetings especially Lisboa, Nice and Stockholm.

The Stockholm European Council focussed on how to modernise the European model and attain the Union's strategic goal for the next decade decided at Lisbon: to become the most competitive and dynamic knowledge-based economy in the world, capable of sustainable economic growth with more and better jobs and greater social cohesion. There was full agreement that economic reform, employment and social policies are mutually reinforcing. Decisions taken must be implemented rapidly and new impetus given to areas where progress has been slow. The open method of coordination was highlighted as an important tool for progress, taking due account of the principles of subsidiarity and proportionality.

The European Council:
- addressed the demographic challenge of an ageing population of which people of working age constitute an ever smaller part;
- discussed how to create more and better jobs, accelerate economic reform, modernise the European social model and harness new technologies;
- issued strategic guidance for the Broad Economic Policy Guidelines in order to achieve sustained growth and stable macroeconomic conditions;
- agreed to improve procedures so that the European Council's Spring meeting will become the focal point for an annual review of economic and social questions. In this context, the Göteborg European Council in June will take account in this review of the generally agreed objective of sustainability;
- agreed to develop ways and means of actively involving the candidate countries in the goals and procedures of the Lisbon strategy.

In table 29 we will compare the eight groups of strategies developed in the Cedefop/ETF project with the most alike strategies formulated in recent EU Meetings.

Table 29: **Comparing strategies at the European level**

STRATEGIES FROM THE CEDEFOP/ETF PROJECT	STRATEGIES FORMULATED IN LISBOA, NICE AND STOCKHOLM
I (Rules regarding) demand articulation	
1 Modern worker strategy	The modernisation of labour markets and labour mobility need to be encouraged to allow greater adaptability to change by breaking down existing barriers. The shift to a knowledge-based economy is of crucial importance for competitiveness and growth and for building a more inclusive society. Despite real progress since Lisbon in the take-up and use of the Internet by businesses, schools and citizens, Europeans are not yet fully using its potential in key areas such as public services, government or commerce.
2 Individual is financially responsible for own training strategy	
II (Rules regarding) supply variety	
1 Flexible providers/ networks of providers strategy	The Commission has announced its intention to propose before the end of the year additional targets for connecting schools to the Internet, to present a communication promoting on-line dispute resolution systems and to support Schola, a Europe-wide action to promote the use of new technologies and develop online school twinning. The European Council notes the interest shown by candidate States in Europe 2002 and looks forward to the Action Plan they will present at the Göteborg European Council setting out how they will embrace these objectives.
2 More training within firms/learning organizations strategy	Improving basic skills, particularly IT and digital skills, is a top priority to make the Union the most competitive and dynamic knowledge-based economy in the world. This priority includes education policies and lifelong learning as well as overcoming the present shortfall in the recruitment of scientific and technical staff. A knowledge-based economy necessitates a strong general education in order to further support labour mobility and lifelong learning

III (Rules regarding) information availability

1 Forecasting strategy

2 Transparency/ availability strategy | The Commission will work with national and local governments, employment services and other relevant actors, to assess before the end of the year the feasibility of establishing a one-stop European mobility information site, in particular by providing employment services with a Europe-wide database on jobs, curricula vitae and learning opportunities.
The Commission intends to present for the 2002 Spring European Council an Action Plan for developing and opening up new European labour markets, as well as specific proposals for a more uniform, transparent and flexible regime of recognition of qualifications and periods of study, as well as on the portability of supplementary pensions, without prejudice to the coherence of Member States' tax systems

IV Coordination (by governments)

1 Monitoring (quality control, free entrance of new providers, counter monopolies) strategy

2 Protection strategy | Regaining full employment not only involves focusing on more jobs, but also on better jobs. Increased efforts should be made to promote a good working environment for all including equal opportunities for the disabled, gender equality, good and flexible work organisation permitting better reconciliation of working and personal life, lifelong learning, health and safety at work, employee involvement and diversity in working life.
Active labour market policies promote social inclusion, which combines the pursuit of social objectives with the sustainability of public finances. Priority should be given by Member States to implementing National Action Plans on combating poverty and social exclusion in order to progress on the basis of the common objectives agreed in Nice, assessed by commonly agreed indicators.

As can be seen from this table the EU strategies don't cover all categories of strategies developed in the Cedefop/ETF project. Especially the categories
- individual is financially responsible for its own training strategy;
- forecasting strategy;
- monitoring (quality control, free entrance of new providers, counter monopolies) strategy,

are more or less empty ones

5. Robustness of strategies vis-à-vis scenarios

We can never really predict the future, so the best strategies are strategies that are relevant in all scenarios (or at least in more than one). These strategies are called robust. Each project team worked out the robustness for their strategies vis-à-vis the scenarios used in their country. Every country used different strategies which made it hard to draw general conclusions about the robustness. One way to compare the robustness of the strategies, is to re-cluster the strategies (see chapter) and then look at the robustness of the clusters. That's what was done for this chapter.

In the tables below one can find the robustness of the clusters. Each main category consisting of two clusters of strategies has it's own table in which the countries are listed with the robustness of the strategies that belong to that cluster. The average of the robustness of the strategies in a cluster, is the robustness for the cluster as a whole. The robustness can vary between 1-3:
  1= least robust
  2= quite robust
  3= very robust
If a country did work out the robustness, but had no strategies in a certain cluster, this was signified with a '-'.

5.1. (Rules regarding) demand articulation

Table 30: Robustness of strategies in the demand clusters

STRATEGY	MODERN WORKER STRATEGY		INDIVIDUAL IS FINANCIALLY RESPONSIBLE FOR OWN TRAINING STRATEGY	
Country	*Strategy*	*Robustness*	*Strategy*	*Robustness*
Europe				
Austria				
Czech Republic	B1	1	B2	3
	C3	2		
Estonia				
Germany				
Greece	B1	2	B2	3
	C3	3		
Luxembourg/ Belgium	B4	2	-	-
Poland	B2	3	C6	1
	C3	2		
	C4	2		
	C7	1		
Slovenia				
United Kingdom	S4	2	S3	3
	S8	1	S9	2
	S11	1		
	S13	1		
Total average		1.77		2.00

The United Kingdom and Poland have relatively many strategies in the modern worker strategy cluster, four in total. Other countries have one or two strategies in this cluster. The scores on robustness are low, only Greece has a strategy in this cluster with score 3. The scores on the individual is financially responsible for own training strategy are all 2 or higher, except for the Polish strategy.

5.2. (Rules regarding) supply variety

Table 31: **Robustness of strategies in the supply clusters**

STRATEGY	FLEXIBLE PROVIDERS/ NETWORKS OF PROVIDERS STRATEGY		MORE TRAINING WITHIN FIRMS/LEARNING ORGANIZATIONS STRATEGY	
Country	Strategy	Robustness	Strategy	Robustness
Europe				
Austria				
Czech Republic	-	-	A1 A3	2 1
Estonia				
Germany				
Greece	-	-	A1 A3	3 2
Luxembourg/ Belgium	A1 B2 B3 C1 C2 C4	2 2 2 2 2 1	A2	3
Poland	A3 C1	2 2	A1 A2 A4 B3 B4 C9	2 3 1 2 2 1
Slovenia				
United Kingdom	S12	-	S1 S10	2 2
Total average		1.88		2.00

Almost all strategies in the flexible providers/networks of providers strategy are from Luxembourg/Belgium. This cluster has a score of 1.88 on robustness. The more training within firms/learning organisation strategy has a score of 2.00. Poland has a high representation in this cluster.

5.3. (Rules regarding) information availability

Table 32: **Robustness of strategies in the information clusters**

STRATEGY	FORECASTING STRATEGY		TRANSPARENCY/ AVAILABILITY STRATEGY	
Country	Strategy	Robustness	Strategy	Robustness
Europe				
Austria				
Czech Republic	A2	3	C1	3
Estonia				
Germany				
Greece	A2	2	C1	2
Luxembourg/ Belgium	A3	2	-	-
Poland	-	-	C8	1
Slovenia				
United Kingdom	-	-	S2 S7	3 3
Total average		2.33		2.40

The forecasting strategy only contains three strategies, but all three have relatively high scores on robustness. The robustness for this cluster is 2.33. The transparency/availability cluster has a score of 2.40. Three strategies in this cluster have a score of 3, the Greek strategy scores 2 on robustness and the Polish strategy 1.

5.4. Coordination

Table 33: Robustness of strategies in the coordination clusters

STRATEGY	MONITORING STRATEGY		PROTECTION STRATEGY	
Country	*Strategy*	*Robustness*	*Strategy*	*Robustness*
Europe				
Austria				
Czech Republic	-	-	B2	3
			B3	3
			C2	2
			C4	1
Estonia				
Germany				
Greece	-	-	B2	3
			B3	2
			C2	2
			C4	2
Luxembourg/ Belgium	-	-	B1	3
Poland	C2	2	B1	1
	C10	1	C5	1
Slovenia				
United Kingdom	-	-	S5	3
			S6	2
Total average		1.50		2.15

The monitoring strategy is almost empty. There are only two Polish strategies in it. The protection strategy on the contrary contains 13 strategies. The robustness for this cluster is 2.15.

Seven countries worked out the robustness for their strategies, but only five used the common format (¹). The robustness of the clusters is therefore based on the data of 5 countries and might not be representative for the group as a whole. The robustness of cluster III.1 and III.2 is quite high, respectively 2.33 and 2.40. Cluster IV.1 is the least robust cluster. It has a score of 1.50.

An overview of all scores on robustness is table 34.

Table 34: **Robustness overall**

CLUSTER OF STRATEGIES		ROBUSTNESS
Demand	Modern worker strategy	1.77
	Individual is responsible for own training strategy	2.00
Supply	Flexible providers/networks of providers strategy	1.88
	More training within firms/learning organisations strategy	2.00
Information	Forecasting strategy	2.33
	Transparency/availability strategy	2.40
Coordination	Monitoring strategy	1.50
	Protection strategy	2.15

(¹) Austria & Germany worked out the robustness for their strategies, but they didn't use the common format. Below you can find their tables on robustness.

Austria Strategies	Scen.I	Scen.II	Scen.III
SA1	1	3	2
SA2	2	3	3
SA3	2	2	1
SB1	1	1	
SB2	2	2	2
SB3	2	3	2
SC1	2	2	2
SC2	2		1
SC3	3		1
SC4	2	2	3
SC5	2		1

Germany Strategies	Scen.I	Scen.II	Scen.III
S1	X	X	2
S2	2	3	2
S3	2	2	3
S4	1	3	2
S5	1	3	2
S6	3 (X)	2	1
S7	2 (X)	3	1
S8	2	3	1
S9	1	2	3
S10	1	2	3
S11	3	2	2
S12	2 (X)	2	2
S13	1	2	3

When we put the scores on robustness together in one table, one can see that the forecasting strategy and the transparency/availability strategy are the most robust strategies. They have a score of respectively 2.33 and 2.40. The protection strategy is also robust with a score of 2.15. The least robust cluster of strategies is the monitoring strategy. It has a score of 1.50. Also relatively low on robustness is the modern worker strategy. With a score of 1.77 it's below average. Most scores are above 2.00.

Table 35: **Robustness and frequency**

CLUSTER OF STRATEGIES	FREQUENCY (POPULARITY)	ROBUSTNESS
Modern worker strategy	26	1.77
Individual is responsible for own training strategy	11	2.00
Flexible providers/ networks of providers strategy	16	1.88
More training within firms/learning organisations strategy	22	2.00
Forecasting strategy	8	2.33
Transparency/availability strategy	9	2.40
Monitoring strategy	3	1.50
Protection strategy	26	2.15

As can be seen in table 35 the categories that contains most strategies, are the modern worker strategy and the protection strategy. 26 strategies fit in these categories. The more training within firms is also a popular category. It contains 22 strategies. The protection strategy is not only mentioned frequently, it also scores high on robustness. Although the modern worker strategy is a popular one, it still has a very low robustness (1.66). And there are also other discrepancies. The transparency/availability strategy for example, only contains 9 strategies, but it has a very high robustness, 2.75. So robustness and popularity are not necessarily correlated.

6. Relevant EU-level actors on strategy and scenario interaction

We developed strategies and scenarios with a 6-step iterative procedure. Step 6 in the iterative procedure of developing scenarios and strategies is a questionnaire sent to experts working on the EU-level. The aim is to see whether the policy makers at EU level are able to work with our scenario/strategy framework. Cedefop and ETF wanted to involve some actors and stakeholders working on the European level, e.g. in the European Commission and other EU-institutions and in EU-level social partner organizations, Committees and advisory bodies, to get their appreciation on the relevance and likelihood of the scenarios and the strategies for European Union level policies of VET and LLL.

The questionnaire consists of three parts (see annex III). In the first part, questions are asked concerning the different strategies. What is relevant at the European level with regard to certain strategies and what else should be done? In the second part the three clusters of scenarios are presented and the experts were asked to add aspects to these clusters which could enhance their relevance for European level de-bates. The third part is about the robustness of the different strategies in relation to their frequency. What can be said about the discrepancies in relevance/frequency and robustness?

We've sent the questionnaire to 180 persons in total. Cedefop and ETF provided names and addresses of relevant stakeholders working on the European level. We've sent the questionnaire by regular mail and by e-mail (if the e-mail address was known) and the respondents could return it by mail, e-mail or fax. We had a total response of 31 questionnaires. This is enough when we consider the purpose of the questionnaire: to see whether the strategies – scenarios could be used and considered as an addition to the repertoire of policy makers at the EU-level.

6.1. Strategies

We asked the respondents what could be done more by EU-authorities vis-à-vis the 8 categories of strategies mentioned in chapter 6.2. Below we summarise suggestions made by the respondents. In some cases several respondents came up with the same strategy. Those strategies can be found in the tables, with their frequency in the right column. Sometimes a strategy was only mentioned once, but was retained as an interesting option. Such strategies are indicated below each of the tables.

Modern worker strategy

Table 36: **What needs to be done on the 'modern worker strategy'**

SUGGESTED STRATEGY ELEMENTS	FREQUENCY
Define a conceptual framework regarding the modern worker	5
Increase mobility	4
Exchange/disseminate good practice	3

Some interesting additional suggestions were made which elaborated on the strategy. These included the following:
- To create a win-win situation between employer and employee in order to get the best results;
- To undertake activities towards raising the prestige of VET (in comparison to higher education);
- Study the relation 'flexible approach – social protection of the employee';
- Developing validation of the non-formal and informal learning;
- To develop an information system that would allow workers at EU level to have fast access to information on the flexible forms of work;
- More funds for LLL;
- Emphasise initiative and entrepreneurship;
- Part- time work and working from home should be supported and mobility of the labour force;
- European authorities should implement a legal framework that can help social partners in introducing flexible rules and practices;
- Ensure that increased part-time working isn't directly related to those in the lowest paid jobs – thus adding to increased erosion of rights/self esteem at the lower levels;

- By influencing Member States so that their tax systems and social expenditures can attack areas of unemployment.

The individual is responsible for his/her own training strategy

Table 37: **What needs to be done on the 'individual is responsible for his/her own training strategy'**

SUGGESTED STRATEGY ELEMENTS	FREQUENCY
Be careful: if the individual is responsible, training is only for the rich	4
Provide financial incentives	3
Provide financial support to individual	3
Exchange/disseminate good practice	3
Nothing	2

Four respondents don't agree with this strategy. Their message is: if the individual is responsible, training is only for the rich. In paragraph 6.2 we ask the respondents what strategy elements they think are needed in the current general EU policy. The answers to this question also show that the individual is responsible for his/her own training strategy isn't considered necessary. Not many people opt for this strategy.

Interesting suggestions made were:
- European format for port-folio;
- To validate skills by social partners and the public employment service;
- To adopt an adequate system that would allow workers to have access to forms of credit capable to efficiently foster the investments in their individual vocational training;
- Teach young adults that they as individuals are responsible for their own LLL;
- Development of learning in communities;
- Promotion of learning vouchers;
- Make this training available to those who DO need it and are willing to take it, but who are given little chances in their home-place or in their working environment.

Flexible providers / networks of providers strategy

Table 38: **What needs to be done on the 'flexible providers/networks of providers strategy'**

SUGGESTED STRATEGY ELEMENTS	FREQUENCY
Be aware of and use European networks	5
Exchange/disseminate good practice	4
Organize working groups/platforms	3
Promote the use of ICT	2
Develop a mixed funding system	2

Interesting suggestions made were:
- Support the development of modern apprenticeship;
- Authorities should outsource educational services. Companies and federations should be able to run educational institutions in agreement with authorities;
- Support local and regional networks;
- Promotion of e-learning assessment and certification. Support for virtual net-works of trainers/providers, awards for best practice. Promotion of 'holistic' quality assurance strategies and initiatives;
- Raise the awareness of those Member States whose academic and administrative systems are too rigid to undertake flexible strategies on VET.

More training within firms/learning organizations strategy

Table 39: **What needs to be done on the 'more training within firms/learning organizations strategy'**

SUGGESTED STRATEGY ELEMENTS	FREQUENCY
Provide financial incentives	8
EU needs to support organizations	8
Lead campaigns	3
Set good examples	3
Nothing	5

The respondents made some interesting suggestions:
- Support a European system for the validation of skills;
- Stronger implementation of lifelong learning;
- Private sector/VET partnerships for innovative practice.

Forecasting strategy

Table 40: **What needs to be done on the 'forecasting strategy'**

SUGGESTED STRATEGY ELEMENTS	FREQUENCY
Provide information	4
Develop prognosis instruments	4
Conduct research	3
Nothing	5

Interesting suggestions that were made:
- Use of the Delphi studies on European level;
- To develop digital portfolio;
- To organize seminars with seniors from organisations that are in charge of implementing prospective policies;
- European authorities can set up a Pan European system of forecasting skills and qualification in order to encourage labour mobility;
- More long term forecasting is necessary to guarantee considered reactions;
- Giving Member States specific guidelines for their Occupational Observatories and recommendations for linking employment, counselling and training activities at Member State level.

Transparency/availability strategy

Table 41: What needs to be done on the 'transparency/availability strategy'

SUGGESTED STRATEGY ELEMENTS	FREQUENCY
Develop an EU standard for the structure of the vocational qualifications	12
Make clear definitions	3
Nothing	2

We received a couple of interesting suggestions:
- Promotion of a kind of 'European education and training currency '(and possible additional 'exchange rates' therefore between member states);
- Create a system for the category 'informal learning' → these diplomas are usually recognized only in a local area;
- Outcome focussed assessment and qualifications. Flexible assessment delivery options, independent of time place and course;
- Strengthen the role and scope of the European Forum for the Transparency of Professional Qualifications.

Monitoring strategy

Table 42: What needs to be done on the 'monitoring strategy'

SUGGESTED STRATEGY ELEMENTS	FREQUENCY
Develop a global monitoring system	4
Establish networks	3
Nothing	7

Interesting suggestions were made as follows:
- Developing data collection and management systems;
- Develop the role of European Observatories having in mind the monitoring of new forms of work;
- Put pressure on government/ministries to provide the necessary information by putting deadlines, e.g. 6 months-reporting;

- Strengthen the role of Member States central governments in order to avoid fragmentation of vocational training policies.

Protection strategy

Table 43: **What needs to be done on the 'protection strategy'**

SUGGESTED STRATEGY ELEMENTS	FREQUENCY
Take measures against social exclusion	9
Increase labour market opportunities	2
Dissemination of good practice	2
Nothing	4

Interesting suggestions that were made are:
- Ensuring general access to training and the labour market;
- To detect the individuals that are liable to lose their job before they do so;
- Support projects to develop adapted measures;
- Ensure that information disseminated to these groups is in clear English and also in various minority languages in the UYK to ensure maximum numbers of people understand;
- Provide Member State specific targeted guidelines on training addressed at institutions that look after groups at risk.

6.2. Scenarios

The respondents were asked whether they recognized the scenarios mentioned in chapter 5.6, as those that policy makers at EU level clearly have in mind. In the table below we indicate which scenarios are considered an option for the policy makers.

Table 44: **Recognizable scenarios?**

SCENARIO	YES	NO	NOT COMPLETELY/ YET
Europe and education: rising high	17	5	5
Europe and education: always ahead	17	7	5
Europe and education: still together	6	18	4
Europe and education: it's worth it	2	21	1

As can been seen in table 43, Europe and education: rising high and Europe and education: always ahead, are the scenarios mostly seen as the ones used by policy makers. More than half the respondents believe that those two scenarios are most used as a reference by policy makers. Our respondents have less confidence in the other two scenarios. Europe and education: still together gets 6 votes, and only 2 respondents consider the Europe and education: it's worth it scenario as one that the policy makers have in mind.

Europe and education: always ahead
This seems to be a scenario that policy makers use when it comes to frames of reference. However, some respondents came up with elements they wanted to add in order to make the scenario more plausible. Several people pointed out that in this scenario social aspects are missing. Not enough attention is being paid to the social dimension and certainly not in comparison to economic issues. Adding such elements however would bring this scenario too near to the Europe and education: rising high scenario.
   Here are some other suggestions that the respondents made in regard to this scenario:
- Training in Europe should include an improvement of 'European Identity' in order to promote the failing integration, the development of an European Education and Labour Area and the improvement of mobility in education, training and labour;
- An element reflecting the objective to ensure a high economic growth in all EU regions;
- Too much effort is given to social matters and to economical efforts;

- Partnership for LLL demands a lot of interest from both the state as well as from companies and trade unions. We need a lot of acceptance and respect from each part;
- Economic competition to be realistic and the necessary one, not fierce;
- Measures to regulate the turnover rate of jobs need to be implemented;
- Investment in training by companies does not seem plausible;
- This scenario is more plausible if we consider the competition process at the worldwide level;
- The weakness of 'the Europe always ahead scenario' is the following: economic growth is non-uniform and so it doesn't correspond to the market driven economy, it's impossible to state that the social flexibility is generally introduced into the work organisation, many enterprises are not operational and are failing. Some European countries don't have a system of education and training based on industry demands for general skills and companies don't have much interest to participate in training;
- I don't agree with the economic privatisation, growth and competition;
- Main point of view is that they have no goals or decision-making strategies, Europe seems more ahead than this scenario;
- The training related arguments sound familiar;
- But is this being realised? This I assume is what is being aimed at;
- It is not very appropriate for all countries and they're at different stages of the development.

Europe and education: rising high
The Europe and education: rising high scenario is also a scenario that is recognized as one that the policy makers at EU level have in mind. Only 16% of the respondents think that this is not the case. This scenario is considered the most idealistic one and this is what our respondents think we should aim for, but according to them there's still a long way to go.

Suggestions that were made for this scenario are:
- Transparency is very important and it has to be for everybody. Guidelines from Europe should have more power. (But economic development is leading. It is not for every country);
- Training demand for in-company training;
  Change: Vocational training schemes by alternation between school and firm are modernized and attractive;
- In the subject of training demand and willingness to invest and life long training, we recognize that both individuals and firms are investors in training. But we think that the government role cannot disappear and that they're one of the financers of the LLL;

- Growth in all sectors – highly unlikely;
- Government intervention is substantial on EU-level – entrepreneurs aren't left free. Economic privatisation doesn't seem to be happening. Social training patterns don't seem to happen. Firms and individual are not both investors in training;
- Suggestion to be added: Social exclusion has to be combated;
- Training to implement not only for current needs, but for the future also; to give people advanced skills;
- Because a balance in privatisation between public and private sector, especially a growth of the importance of the private sector, is absolutely necessary for economic competition;
- No suggestions with regard to economic competition, social work-training pat-terns, social organisation of labour and new transferable skills and competencies. The dual system is not 'all and end all'. This is only one form of the vocational training needing clear and accurate rules for enterprises interested in the VET-system.

Europe and education: still together

About one fourth of the respondents consider this scenario as a policy frame, whereas the other 75% don't think this is used as such. There's a tendency to believe that this is our present situation, and some even believe we're beyond this scenario. In this scenario the economic development is in the focus and should be further stimulated and promoted.

Here are the suggestions that were made regarding this scenario:
- Restructuring initiatives should be more precise. Employment development should be more evident;
- Some problems need to be overcome. Social work patterns influence training;
- This scenario seems the result of an uncertainty situation that lack of precise direction and aims.

Europe and education: it's worth it

This scenario is seen least as a policy context. Almost 90% of the respondents think the policy makers don't have this in mind. If countries regard this as a frame of reference, there'll be a great delay in progress. According to the respondents it's a conservative scenario, with a lack of unity. Hardly any suggestions were done with regard to elements that needed to be added in order to make the scenario more plausible at EU level.

The two suggestions that were made are stated below:
- Flexibility – encourage initiative enterprise. Mobility;

- Economy first and in cooperation.

Europe and education: always ahead and Europe and education: rising high are both scenarios that are seen as frames of reference for policy makers at the EU-level. The respondents consider the other two scenarios less interesting, because they're too pessimistic. Europe and education: still together is referred to as the present situation and Europe and education: it's worth it is too conservative according to the respondents. That scenario will slow down Europe from further development.

6.3. Robustness

In chapter 7 we discussed the robustness of the strategies. A robust strategy is a strategy that works well in more than one scenario. The more scenarios it fits, the more robust it is. No matter what the future will look like, a strategy is appropriate when it's robust in several –preferable all- scenarios. It's safe to implement a strategy that's robust. In this project it turned out that some strategies were given more attention than others. Apparently those strategies were considered important, but are they also robust?

In some cases a strategy scored highly in importance, but scored low on robustness. For example: the modern worker strategy is a popular one, but it has a very low robustness (1.77). Is it a wise decision to implement such a strategy? There are also other discrepancies. The transparency strategy for example, only contains 9 strategies, but it has a high degree of robustness (2.40). The individual is responsible for own training is also a very robust strategy and so is the protection strategy. These results can be found in table 34.

We asked the respondents if at the European level they observed the same discrepancies between the popularity and the robustness of the strategies. They could answer with true or false. Below table 45 gives the observations of the respondents. The strategies are ranked. The first strategy in the table is the one of which most respondents said it was true that there's a discrepancy.

Table 45: **Popularity compared to robustness**

STRATEGY ELEMENTS	TOO POPULAR IN REGARD TO ROBUSTNESS			
	True	Ranking	False	Ranking
Modern worker strategy	14	1	7	7
Protection	13	2	8	6
More training within firms	13	2	9	5
Individual is financially responsible	12	3	11	3
Forecasting	11	4	10	4
Flexible providers strategy	9	5	12	2
Transparency	8	6	12	2
Monitoring	6	7	15	1

As can be seen in Table 45, there's a correlation between the true and false column. The more people observed a discrepancy and answered with 'true', the less people answered 'false'. The modern worker strategy is number 1 in the true ranking and number 7 in the false ranking. And with the monitoring strategy, not many discrepancies are observed, so there's a low score on true and a high score on false. In this table the scores of the true and false column are almost each other's opposite. So far, there's a considerable consistency in the respondents answers.

What elements are needed in the overall EU policy in the field of training/LLL? The respondents could choose between the 8 strategies mentioned before. The strategies were scored as follows: 3 points if it was mentioned at the first place, 2 points for the second place and 1 point for the third place. Four strategies are mentioned very often, while the other 4 are mentioned remarkably less. If we don't attach a weight to the scores and give each mentioned strategy 1 point, the same 4 strategies rank highest. The differences between the middle strategies become less significant, however. Table 46 shows the scores on the strategies, their ranking and the times they were mentioned at the first place.

Table 46: **Strategy elements needed in the EU policy in the field of training/LLL**

STRATEGY ELEMENTS	SCORE	RANKING	FIRST PLACE	RANKING
Transparency	37	1	6	3
Flexible providers strategy	35	2	7	2
Modern worker strategy	31	3-4	9	1
More training within firms	31	3-4	1	6
Individual is financially responsible	13	5-6	4	4
Protection	13	5-6	2	5
Forecasting	11	7	-	-
Monitoring	3	8	-	-

The following strategies are considered to be most appropriate for the general EU policy: transparency, flexible providers, modern worker and more training within firms (see table 46) Three of these strategies are mentioned often at the first place. The more training within firms strategy has a high score, but was only mentioned once at the first place. The transparency strategy is regarded as a robust strategy. It has a score of 2.40 (on a scale of 1-3). It's thus a good decision to implement this strategy. The other three strategies that are considered to fit best with the policy of the EU in the area of training and LLL are less robust (modern worker 1.77, flexible providers 1.88, more training within firms 2.00). In fact, they have the three lowest scores of all strategies on robustness.

We asked the respondents how they would name the policy they preferred to see on EU-level. This is what they came up with.

Preferred policy names at EU-level:
- Competitive Europe
- Maximum opportunities policy
- A competency based society
- Giving means to flexibility
- Flexible/transparency/protection (FTP) strategy
- Jointly responsible education and training
- FIT Europe (forecasting, individual is responsible, transparency)

- General up-skilling policy
- Flexible LLL
- LLL
- Balanced growth policy
- A true European value
- Development and responsibility for coordination in a flexible way
- Employee based policy
- European modern worker and protection
- Flexible training and LLL
- Individual and firm cooperation
- European Development
- Policy of clear rules, social justness and equal opportunities
- Democratic, foreseeing, social responsible and economic developing
- Flexibility and transparency in LLL

As one can see, life long learning is a recurrent theme and so is flexibility. Transparency and protection are also important factors.

The respondents were asked with which scenario their preferred policy fitted best. The following ranking was chosen most: Europe and education: rising high; Europe and education: always ahead; Europe and education: still together; Europe and education: it's worth it. This sequence was given by 33% of the respondents. 16 % switched the first two scenarios and ranked them like this: Europe and education: always ahead; Europe and education: rising high; Europe and education: still together; Europe and education: it's worth it.

Almost 14% considered 'still together' more apt than 'always ahead' and they came up with: Europe and education: rising high; Europe and education: still together; Europe and education: always ahead; Europe and education: it's worth it.

The other respondents used different varieties, either with 'always ahead' or 'rising high' first. Only one respondent considered 'still together' fitting best with his/her preferred policy. A combination of 'Europe and education: always ahead' and 'Europe and education: rising high' (in either order) at the first and second place, was mentioned by 18 respondents. We called this group A. Only 7 respondents (group B) didn't give this combination a high ranking. In table 46 one can see the strategies that group A and B consider to be needed.

Table 47: **Important strategies**

	Group A		Group B	
Strategy	Frequency	Percentage	Frequency	Percentage
Transparency	14	26	5	24
More training	11	20	3	14
Flexible (networks of) providers	10	19	3	14
Modern worker	6	11	4	19
Forecasting	5	9	1	5
Protection	4	7	3	14
Individual is financially responsible for own training	3	6	-	-
Monitoring	1	2	2	10

The 18 respondents of group A consider the transparency strategy as most important. The more training within firms strategy and the flexible providers strategy also score high, in contrast to the monitoring strategy and the individual is financially responsible strategy. Respectively 2% and 6% of the respondents consider these strategies as relevant. Group B, the group that doesn't consider the combination of 'Europe rising high' and 'Europe always ahead' as the two scenarios that fit best with their wished policy, values the transparency strategy high too. This group considers the modern worker strategy also as a needed strategy, whereas group A thinks this one is less important. The same can be said about the protection strategy.

The final part of the questionnaire consisted of questions on the overarching scenarios developed by Cedefop. Those results can be found in Annex IV.

6.4. Concluding remarks

When we look at the overall results, we can conclude that some scenarios are considered more as a frame of reference than others. Europe and education: always ahead and Europe and education: rising high are the most dominant scenarios. More than half the respondents believe that those two scenarios are most used as a reference by policy makers. The other 2 scenarios are considered too pessimistic.

Within these scenarios we can allocate strategies that could be useful. According to the respondents the following strategy elements are needed in the EU policy in the field of training and LLL: the transparency strategy, the flexible (networks of) providers strategy, the modern worker strategy and the more training within firms strategy. When we compare these results to the market model (see chapter 6.2 and figure 8) it can be seen that the coordination category is under-represented. The transparency strategy belongs to the information cluster, the modern worker strategy to the supply cluster and the flexible providers and more training within firms strategy to the demand cluster. This means that none of the strategies in the coordination cluster is often mentioned. Apparently the respondents don't value the monitoring or the protection strategy a lot. There's a preference for the demand cluster. Both strategies in this cluster are considered useful.

The model 'market coordination by government' (Figure 1)

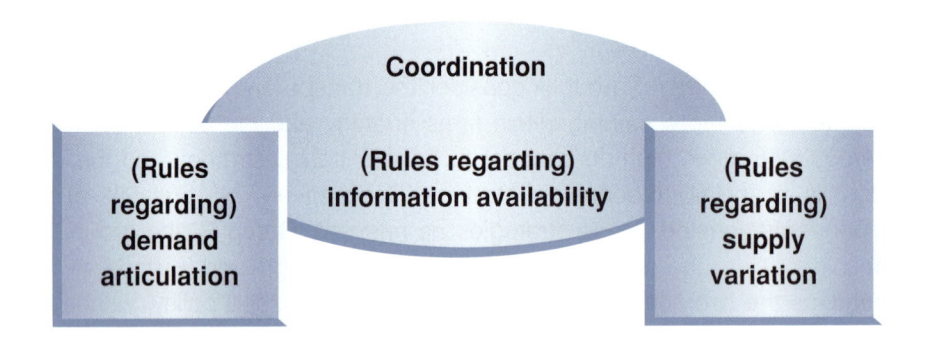

Coordination

(Rules regarding) demand articulation

(Rules regarding) information availability

(Rules regarding) supply variation

Earlier we stated that robust strategies are the best strategies. They can be used in more than one scenario and are thus 'safer' than strategies that are only appropriate in one scenario. In chapter 7 we tested our strategies on robustness. Those results can be found in table 34. What we're interested in now, is to see whether the strategies that are needed in the overall EU policy are also the most robust strategies. In the table below (table 48) the popularity of the strategies is compared to their robustness. A strategy is popular when many respondents believe it should be implemented, when they consider it important. The robustness varies between 1-3. 1 = least robust 2= quite robust 3= very robust. The scores on popularity are taken from table 45.

Table 48: **Strategies: scores on popularity and robustness**

STRATEGY	SCORE	ROBUSTNESS
Transparency	37	2.40
Flexible providers	35	1.88
Modern worker	31	1.77
More training within firms	31	2.00
Individual is financially responsible	13	2.00
Protection	13	2.15
Forecasting	11	2.33
Monitoring	3	1.50

The transparency strategy is considered important and it's a very robust strategy with a score of 2.40. In fact, it's the most robust strategy. It would be a good decision to implement this strategy. The more training within firms is also an important and robust strategy. The other 2 strategies the respondents thought were needed are less robust. The forecasting strategy is a very robust strategy, but the respondents don't mention this strategy a lot when it comes to strategies that are needed in EU policy.

7. The scenario method

7.1. The method as used in this project

The method used in this project has been described in paragraph 4.1. In a more detailed version the method contains 22 steps. We present these 22 steps here below.

Table 49: **22 steps**

1	Defining the scope and the key questions.
2	Identifying the major stakeholders.
3	Identifying basic trends.
4	Identifying basic strategy elements.
5	Identifying key uncertainties, driving forces.
6	Classification of the main developments according to importance and uncertainty. Aim is to find the two major developments that are the most important as well as most uncertain.
7	Constructing initial scenario themes and matrices.
8	Developing scenarios. General themes emerge from the simple scenarios and from checking them. Although the trends appear in all the scenarios, they can be given more or less weight or attention in different scenarios. At this stage not all scenarios need to be fleshed out.
9	Checking for consistency and plausibility.
10	Are there trends compatible within the chosen time frame?
11	Do the scenarios combine outcomes of uncertainties that indeed go together?
12	Are the major stakeholders placed in positions they do not like and can change?
13	Evolving toward scenarios and robust strategies.
14	Next we retrace the previous steps and see if the scenarios and strategies address the real issues facing the national VET-system.

15	Are the scenarios relevant to have impact, the scenarios should connect directly with the mental maps and concerns of the users.
16	Are the scenarios internally consistent and perceived as such?
17	Are the scenarios archetypal? They should describe generally different futures rather than variations on one theme.
18	Are the scenarios describing an equilibrium, or a state in which the system might exist for some length of time?
19	Test robustness of strategies in different scenarios.
20	Strategic conversation: To develop these scenarios and strategies a strategic conversation should have taken place. 'It is the general conversational process by which people influence each other, the decision taking and the longer term pattern in institutional action and behaviour'.The national seminars were partly set up for this purpose.
21	Institutionalisation: 'Ultimately the most effective way to ensure institutional effective-ness of the scenario process is for management to make the scenarios part of the on-going formal decision making process'. The scenarios have to become part of the sys-tem for discussing strategic questions.
22	Confronting experts with the strategies – scenarios combinations to see whether the method really enriches their repertoire.

7.2. Experiences with the method

The project partners were asked to give comments on the scenario method in general and on this specific project. Their comments could be classified in the following categories: education and human resource development, getting the data, beyond the short term, European impact and actors and implementation.

7.2.1. Education and human resource development

Coordinating human resource development
The ensuing comments were aimed at possible VET development variants. They took into account in particular European trends, for example the conclusions from the meeting of the OECD countries ministers of education, but also the outputs of other expert teams dealing with scenarios in the Czech envi-

ronment (for example the scenario of the government project the 'Visions of the Czech Republic development till 2015'). The attention paid by Cedefop and ETF to the prognoses and comparisons was highly appreciated as well as the possible influence of the Scenario Project results on the education policy in individual participating countries. In particular suggestions to establish a multi-subject management body co-ordinating the activities of institutions concerned with human resources development, recommendations regarding lifelong learning and suggestions to strengthen the position of regions in initial and continuing VET were supported in the discussion about strategies in the Czech environment. (Czech Republic)

Human resource strategy
A key aspect that is underplayed in both the strategy and the scenario statements is the role of human resource strategies. It is a matter of debate whether these should be incorporated into the narratives of the scenarios or into the subject matter for strategy development. The HR policies of public and private organisations, of large firms and SMEs have a crucial role to play, involving both the organisation of work and the quality, content and availability of training. We sought little information on HRD, and this is a significant weakness in the method that the whole project has used to date. (United Kingdom)

Experts used to transfer specialisations
VET takes on a considerable interest in Luxembourg where the concept of lifelong learning is omnipresent. Many experts have already looked into this field by trying to give answers to the evolutions of the Luxembourg society. It is within this framework that we think that the scenarios method is of a particular interest as it allows to get an anticipation process more than a response to existing phenomena. (Luxembourg/Belgium)

7.2.2. Getting the data

Use of interviewing
Experts were primarily involved in the form of structured interviews which lasted on average for 1.5 hours. The interview had two principal aims: first, to get qualitative information on basic factors and strategies identified and agreed upon in Phase 1 to be used in scenarios creation; and second, further development of initial scenarios based on the common scenarios framework. Since the participating experts had varying degrees of competence, they concentrated on those basic factors that they had better knowledge of. The interviews

first took place in the form of individual interviews. What followed were correction of scenarios, group interviews and scenarios workshops. The most difficult methodological step was the integration of results of interviews into scenarios framework. (Estonia)

Quantitative descriptors
Often the experts limited themselves to the present only and were inclined to talk about the existing situation and existing problems; it was much more difficult to make them speak of different possible futures. What seemed to be particularly cumbersome was anticipation of descriptors of quantitative indicators in the con-text of different scenarios. On the other hand, experts tended to speak extensively of normative things: what would be the desirable/necessary state of affairs, what should be done and were often trapped in numerous details. (Estonia)

Availability of statistics
For a number of reasons, like absence of long statistical time series (the entire statistics-collection system was disrupted in the late 1980s formally as well as methodologically; comparative data were again made available not earlier than in 1989), deficit of 'hard'/numerically expressed data and surveys, weak traditions of traditional prognostics and other limitations, it was particularly hard to assess in quantitative terms different dimensions involved in scenarios. It is somewhat easier to do it in the economic context. (Estonia)

Outside the box
The next stage was to involve both researchers and policy players in England, Scotland and Northern Ireland in a series of interviews to explore the intersection of a number of strategies with the different scenarios. Our interviewees, like the participants in the final UK seminar, experienced these discussions as engaging and as helpful in thinking beyond short-term imperatives - 'outside the box', as several colleagues put it to us. In consequence, we have been able to identify five clusters of strategies that will each carry a different weight dependant on the scenario that actually develops, as well as a set of strategies that are likely to be robust across all of the scenarios. (United Kingdom)

7.2.3. Beyond the short term

Long term perspective
The methodology succeeds in helping experts and policy makers to look at strategies against the template of different scenarios. This helps policy making to look beyond the short-term perspective and to weigh up longer-term possibilities and risks. Clustering the strategies helps this process, and is capable of providing valuable indications for action.

   A danger inherent in the method is that it could provide rather broad generalisations that do not, in the event, help to take the strategic analysis forward. However, the way in which the project had succeeded in examining particular strategies in the context of different scenarios indicates that it had proved possible to reach some conclusions about the agents involved in each of the strategies, and to begin to reach conclusions about the likely actions involved in implementation. (Given re-sources and a wish on the part of policy makers to engage further, we could develop this aspect in the aftermath of the seminar.) (United Kingdom)

Strategies
With regard to the strategies, particularly the four which are most essential for Greece, the view was expressed that in effect they constitute a package of options which can be implemented separately, and with different impacts on all three scenarios, functioning to a degree independently of the scenarios in the sense that they can prevent specific situations contained in the scenarios. (Greece)

Elements of more than one scenario
Another observation regards the relation of several elements between the three different scenarios, and that the means of distinguishing them serves methodological requirements only. Most probably, elements of more than one scenario will appear in the development of Greek society in the coming decade.

   In any case, reservations were generally expressed, even by those who voiced an opinion regarding the likelihood of scenarios becoming predominant, precisely be-cause they contain a degree of schematisation, but mainly because many elements of the scenarios are bound up with each other. Reservations were also expressed with regard to the functionality of the scenarios, which do have a common methodological basis but concern different levels of development of European countries. (Greece)

Alternatives awareness
The main difficulty at the time of this project was to go beyond the vision and the perception of the current tendencies in the country, in order to give a large place to uncertainty, major component of the scenarios method. Our aim was not to imagine the future consequences of the current trends but to bring alternatives to them. (Luxembourg/Belgium)

Perception of scenarios or stages or paths
Since the developments in the technological level of the economy, organisational culture, level of vocational schools and their management as well as in other relevant fields have been highly uneven and unequal in different sectors of the economy, different regions, different vocational schools etc in Estonia, the experts, as a rule, recognised the 'germs' of all the scenarios as they appear today and termed the scenarios generally 'probable and robust'. At the same time in some cases they perceived the proposed scenarios as different stages rather than alternative paths of development. (Estonia)

Spill over effects
The project has already led to several associated developments: scenarios work to look at qualifications needs among a small number of national training organisations, an exploration of scenarios and strategies for the development of the school curriculum and assessment in England; the possibility of drawing out more detailed policy implications for training with policy makers who attended the April 2001 seminar; a pilot for the city of Barcelona to see how forecasting and scenarios techniques can be combined to anticipate and meet future training needs in a modern, changing European city. (United Kingdom)

7.2.4. European impact

Endogenous national potential
The problem was identified of the adequacy of the endogenous potential in the country's political and social system, so that the most suitable package of measures (strategies) can be chosen, with the aim of giving an impetus to society, which appears to be slow in responding to the effects of the economy. What is occurring is the exogenous support (see EU) of the endogenous potential, so that systematised objectives are met, the primary one being the connection of development policies with employment and training policies. In this context, the likelihood of there being a great variety of forms of employment, levels of pay and different forms of integration of individuals in the work

environment cannot be ignored, so that the present typical model of paid employment may decline significantly. (Greece)

European context
During the analytical discussion, two elements predominated:
A   The relation of the likely alternative scenarios with the Greek economy and social reality, and
B   The likely strategies, whose implementation corresponds to/or influences the scenarios.

The view was expressed by several participants that the course taken by the Greek economy and society is significantly bound up with the developments and the more general choices of the European Union and with Europe's rate of social and economic development; this is something that also determines the scenarios.

In the area of employment and vocational training, the general directions are taking shape to a greater and greater extent on the supranational level. This also deter-mines the national strategies to an important degree. (Greece)

Effect of European Union
Poland's accession to the European Union will have a significant importance for the development of the Polish vocational education and training system. It will al-low for a full inclusion of Poland in the European cooperation networks and for the use of financial resources of the European Social Fund. Problems relating to a future EU membership and, in particular, to the transition periods for Polish workforce mobility suggested by the EU countries (Austria, Germany) were indicated. An opinion was expressed that, in practice, the limitations resulting from the transition periods will be omitted in the case of highly qualified workers which may lead to a 'brain drain' reducing the country's development potential. It will mainly be the case of a development following the first scenario. (Poland)

7.2.5. Actors and implementation

Implementation of strategies
The development of Polish vocational education and training system requires a more extensive involvement of employers in the implementation of adequate strategies. However, there are still the following obstacles:
- labour market situation - high unemployment level resulting in a large supply of a highly qualified workforce, which makes the employers become little interested in investments in training;

- legal regulations discouraging the employers from getting involved in the education and training sphere;
- lack of understanding among the employers for the educational system and, in particular, a vocational education reform. (Poland)

Roles of the State, institutions, associations and individuals
A weakening of community ties, a more-or-less continuous revolution in ICT capacity, and the uncertainty of global change mean two things for the state. Firstly, that in terms of qualifications and the up-dating of frameworks for training provision, the modern state has to lead change to create a fast turn around, and this is difficult to achieve. Secondly, these wider changes tend to create a 'catch-as-catch-can' situation - with continuing, even growing, tension between good access for some and denial of access to others. Even in this 'mass individualisation' future, access to the technology would be uneven. Here, furthermore, the state would have to continue to play an important role. This suggests that there will be an uneasy co-existence of the goals of competitiveness and social policy. (United Kingdom)

7.3. Improvement of the method

In order to analyse the experiences of the project teams with the method, the countries were asked to fill in a three columns format. The first column was called 'steps as suggested at the start of the project'. This column was filled in by Max Goote Expert Centre. The second column 'Steps as actually taken in your project' and the third column 'Steps as you see them in the ideal situation based on your experiences' had to be filled in by the countries. Especially the third column is interesting. One of the aims of this project is to inspire others to use the scenario method. This report contains a description of the methodology, how things were done in this project. The last column gives suggestions of what could be done better/differently in future studies. Below you can find an overview of their suggestions in regard to each of the 22 steps in the project. Similar suggestions are marked *. At the end of each suggestion, you can find the country reporting that particular experience.

1. **Defining the scope and key questions**
   - *Small seminar with key players (United Kingdom)
   - *Discussion with external experts (Czech Republic)
   - *Include into initial discussions experts and stakeholders (Poland)

- More time (Germany)
- More use of ICT platforms (Germany)

2. Identifying the major stakeholders
- Identify complete list of stakeholders and the group them (United Kingdom)
- Define a restricted list or group of key actors involved in the field of VET policies (Luxembourg/Belgium)
- Introduce theoretical sampling (Germany)
- More representative selection (Poland)

3. Identifying basic trends
- *Optimal (United Kingdom)
- *Additional desk research enabled to discuss certainties and uncertainties once more (Czech Republic)
- *Optimal (Poland)
- More time (Germany)
- Use of ICT platforms (Germany)
- Ask each expert to deal with each trend and then to link them with each other (Luxembourg/Belgium)

4. Identifying basic strategy elements
- *Elements must be clustered into maximum of 6 strategies for action (clusters of strategies) (United Kingdom)
- *Lower number of grouped strategies (Czech Republic)
- *Dealing with a more restricted number of strategies (6-8) would have been more efficient (Luxembourg/Belgium)
- Clusters need to be tested for clarity before use (United Kingdom)
- Avoid stating the obvious as strategies (United Kingdom)
- Senior players need to identify strategy elements strong ownership to key players (United Kingdom)
- More time (Germany)
- More use of ICT platforms (Germany)
- More active participation of external experts. Their role in the interviews was rather passive. They commented on proposed strategies but very rarely proposed new ones (Poland)

5. Identifying key uncertainties, driving forces
- Isolate the major areas of diverse opinion. Axes which show major diversity in opinion need to be listed in order of strength of diverse opinion. The

list then needs to be reduced to 4 or 5 elements. The scenarios should be build around these elements. (United Kingdom)
- Method of using contingency tables is too mechanistic. It misses the main point of creating plausible but challenging scenarios. (United Kingdom)
- This preparatory step for the construction of mega scenarios should be based on the deep expertises and a follow up discussion on the main factors and their influence → increase rate of objectivity. (Czech Republic)
- Add question on desirability (especially to identify driving forces) (Germany)
- *Additional verification/comments by external experts. (Poland)
- *A good way to identify robust key uncertainties and driving forces could be to intermingle experts' standpoints and outcomes of desk researchers. (Luxembourg/Belgium)

6. **Classification of the main developments according to importance and uncertainty. Aim is to find two 2 major developments that are most important as well as most uncertain**
    - The most appropriate participants must undertake serious analysis of the findings, then take an imaginative step. (United Kingdom)
    - Identification of major developments would be easier if the discussion of experts would be based on the provisional matrix of supposed main factors and their possible reflections. (Czech Republic)
    - Classification/factor analysis might be easier when using more one-dimensional, pure and also more polarising trend-items in the standardised instrument. (Germany)
    - The most uncertain trends would possibly be better identified by looking deeper into the distribution of trend ratings. (Germany)
    - It was optimal within the taking into account the existing limitations and constraints. (Poland)

7. **Constructing initial scenario themes and matrices**
    - This step is optimal. (United Kingdom)
    - Future respondents from interviews could be involved, to prevent later need of reformulation. (Czech Republic)
    - Involving the experts in the phase of building of the first provisional scenarios would have prevent the team from wasting time with reformulation. (Luxembourg/Belgium)
    - Classification/factor analysis might be easier when using more one-dimensional, pure and also more polarising trend-items in the standardised instrument. (Germany)

- The most uncertain trends would possibly be better identified by looking deeper into the distribution of trend ratings. (Germany)
- To focus the national seminar more on scenarios than on methodology as it was the case. (Poland)

8. **Developing scenarios. General view on scenario. At this stage not all scenarios need to be fleshed out**
   - Make sure that strategic statements do not creep in to the scenarios. (United Kingdom)
   - Make sure that scenarios describe the demand site of training and not the supply side. (United Kingdom)
   - All respondents received set of supporting materials and full text of the provisional scenarios before. (Czech Republic)
   - The implementation of a standardised tool could be useful in this case. (Luxembourg/Belgium)

9. **Checking for consistency and plausibility**
   - Step seemed optimal. (United Kingdom)
   - We need a sampling process to make sure al major stakeholders have a chance to comment on: plausibility, clarity, challenge, consistency between scenarios and missing elements. (United Kingdom)
   - More representative verification. (Poland)
   - A wide survey about consistency and plausibility would have been relevant. (Luxembourg/Belgium)
   - The preliminary cooperation with respondents as describe in point 7 would rationalise the procedure of scenario modification. (Czech Republic)

10. **Are there trends compatible within the chosen time frame?**
    - We need a sampling process to make sure al major stakeholders have a chance to comment on: plausibility, clarity, challenge, consistency between scenarios and missing elements. (United Kingdom)
    - *The preliminary cooperation with respondents as describe in point 7 would rationalise the procedure of scenario modification. (Czech Republic)
    - *Future respondents from interviews could be involved, to prevent later need of reformulation. (Czech Republic)
    - 20 years would enhance the willingness of experts and interviewees to abstain from short-term restraints. (Germany)

- A narrower timeframe (5 years) could allow to define a more predictable aspect of the scenarios. (Luxembourg/Belgium)

11. **Do the scenarios combine outcomes of uncertainties that indeed go together?**
    - *The preliminary cooperation with respondents as describe in point 7 would rationalise the procedure of scenario modification. (Czech Republic)
    - *Future respondents from interviews could be involved, to prevent later need of reformulation. (Czech Republic)

12. **Are the major stakeholders placed in positions they do not like and can change?**
    - Respondents must be given a strong element of decision as to which aspect of the matrix they concentrate on - interviewing about scenarios they find implausible or strategies concerning which they have no interest defeat the purpose. (United Kingdom)
    - *Avoiding this question (on desirability) makes it different to get answers on this question, question of desirability should be touched. (Germany)
    - *Respondents should be given more direct questions related to this issue. (Poland)

13. **Evolving toward scenarios and robust strategies**
    - *Make sure the presentation of the scenarios is taken seriously. It affects greatly the processes which follow by optimising engagement of the stakeholder. (United Kingdom)
    - *Propose a description as much credible as possible of the various scenarios. (Luxembourg is placed in a situation of important stability on many points such as economy, social, etc, what made the construction of alternative scenarios delicate). (Luxembourg/Belgium)

14. **Next we retrace the previous steps and see if the scenarios and strategies address the real issues facing the national VET-systems**
    - *Engage with policy makers and researchers in a practical exercise that meets their on-going needs. We are trying to do this elsewhere. (United Kingdom)
    - *Define common works getting together experts and political decision makers. The success and consensus found in this respect depends on the degree of implication of the various actors (Luxembourg/Belgium)

- Parallel scenario building in which national and transnational questions and issues alternate in the process of scenario-building. (Germany)
- Web-based Metadata management systems could be a possibility of handling the flood of information. (Germany)
- The project follow-up which would enable such testing. (Poland)

15. **Are the scenarios relevant. To have impact, the scenarios should con-nect directly with the mental maps and concerns the users**
    - To foresee appropriate follow-up of the project. (Poland)

16. **Are the scenarios internally consistent and perceived as such?**
    - *Ongoing adaptation and amendment. (United Kingdom)
    - *To foresee appropriate follow-up of the project. (Poland)
    - *Progressive adaptation and refinement. (Luxembourg/Belgium)

17. **Are the scenarios archetypal? They should describe generally different futures rather than variations on one theme**
    - To foresee appropriate follow-up of the project. (Poland)

18. **Are the scenarios describing an equilibrium, or a state in which the system might exist for some length of time?**
    - Be clear on this point at the outset. (United Kingdom)
    - To foresee appropriate follow-up of the project. (Poland)

19. **Test robustness of strategies in different scenarios**
    - *The steps were effective, but with fewer strategies the whole process would have been easier and more reliable. (United Kingdom)
    - *The number of strategies should have been limited. The respondents should have got them in the clustered form and not divided by contexts as it was done. (Poland)
    - The discussion of actors and instruments needs to be given a stronger place in interview schedules. (United Kingdom)
    - Suggestion: maybe the manual can have a few sample interview schedules to show the practicalities of doing things like this. (United Kingdom)
    - Interviews on the basis of the results (Luxembourg/Belgium)

20. **Strategic conversation. To develop....behaviour. The national seminars were partly set up for this purpose**
    - *Don't introduce other subjects in the seminar. (United Kingdom)
    - *To focus the national seminar more on this issue. (Poland)

- *The seminar structure needs to built around strategic conversations more effectively. Structure in group work ➤ let us work up the more detailed actions entailed. (United Kingdom)
- It's necessary to ensure for the process to continue, in a middle and long-term horizon of VET development. (Czech Republic)

21. **Institutionalisation: Ultimately....process. The scenarios have to become part of the system for discussing strategic questions**
    - *The scenario building, strategic conversation and on-going adaptation of the method, including the involvement of the researcher with the policy making process should be on-going. (United Kingdom)
    - *The process should be permanent and not limited to one-off undertakings. (Poland)
    - The establishment of the multisubject management of VET. The exchange of information on VET development would be an integral part of the decision making places of this new coordinating body. (Czech Republic)

22. **Confronting experts with the strategy – scenario combinations to see whether the method really enriches their repertoire**
    - Step 22 is reported in chapter 8

7.4. Conditions for application

7.4.1. Open planning

Interaction between systems
The use of the scenario approach in an extremely fast-changing and complex environment, which is the specific case of CEE transition countries, is particularly appropriate for a variety of reasons: 1) the method enables to reduce the steadily growing uncertainty 2) to use a systematic approach in VET planning whereby taking into consideration the economic and social environment of VET development. This is not a common practice in designing development plans either for VET or the economy in our country. In traditional planning practices, also relative to VET, the systems are predominantly treated as isolated entities without much attention being paid to their interaction. The latter, however, critically influences the way the system develops. (Estonia)

Learning from each other
The scenario method further makes it possible to integrate different visions of the future by engaging experts with diverse backgrounds. The scenario creation itself was mostly an exercise permitting extensive learning from each other for all the ex-perts involved in the implementation of the project. (Estonia)

Transversal relationships
The implementation of the scenarios method in the context of VET comprises a stake and a particular interest if we consider that it is dependent from other fields which influence its evolution (economy, technology, labour and employment). Thus, for the particular context of Luxembourg, it was especially easy to reconcile these various aspects if we take into account that the size of the country implies that the questioned experts had necessarily transverse competences in the various fields. The particular situation of the country has also constrained us to direct our study in a somewhat different manner, by having recourse to a necessarily restricted number of experts, which all have wide responsibilities in the various fields concerned. (Luxembourg/Belgium)

Broadening perspectives
The attraction of using scenarios in the context of VET, and its main distinguishing feature, is that it can take minds of planners into a new place. They can loosen the grip of the 'here and now' for long enough to get a different perspective of the future. As one of our experts said: 'It is like taking the telescope into the future and looking back to the present to see what we could be doing now to prepare for the future'. Most of our experts enjoyed the process of doing this and thought it a useful exercise. The second feature which people found useful was that scenarios methodology does not dodge the uncertainties, it faces them head on. Forecasting tends to minimise uncertainty and is therefore limited in its scope for prediction. We found that making scenarios a story which springs from the facts of today and current forecasts seems to make them all the more plausible as futures. (United Kingdom)

7.4.2. Learning instrument for policy makers

Different agencies apply scenarios
Whilst the findings are based on limited evidence they give a flavour of what can be determined in the face of uncertainty. The methodological dissemination is probably more important. If a concerted effort can be made to develop fairly sophisticated scenarios for the future -at European, UK and perhaps

more localised levels- then different agencies can apply effort to develop strategies relevant to their work in optimising the effect of VET. (United Kingdom)

New aspects of the methodology
Finally, participants expressed the opinion that the method used in the project breaks new ground. In doing so, it has something in common with other innovative approaches that we see developing at the moment. It engages both research and policy making; it is interdisciplinary; it takes uncertainty about the future into ac-count. In policy terms, the scenarios approach should help to identify, for example, when and how the government should intervene, and help clarify issues about the balance between competition/competitiveness and social inclusion in the policy making and implementation process. (United Kingdom)

Broad range of parallel scenario work
The possibility of developing a broad range of parallel scenario work was suggested as one of the ways to develop the ideas under discussion at the seminar. This would involve a distinction between the dynamics of initial and continuing training, and a focus on different settings in terms of training, market infiltration and the scale and characteristics of workplace organisation. Work can be done, potentially, at the macro and micro level, and on different timescales, and this should involve links with work being conducted by others. From this point of view the end product is, for some purposes, less important than the engagement in dialogue. (United Kingdom)

Sociological imagination
Altogether the scenarios were found to be to multidimensional in their scope and not fitted with the necessary degree of plausibility, this sometimes made the discussion somewhat complex. The analysis of comments and further analysis might compensate those lacks of the initial findings. Others stated a domination by main-stream-trends and missed the exhaustion of sociological fantasy for scenario-construction, which might have led to lower degree of binding force of the scenarios. However, the discussion process was appreciated and the potential for further scenario-construction attested. As an important side-effect the project might also increase the awareness of German actors for the European field which is almost and end for itself. A clear appeal was made to describe the background of the study from the data collection to scenario-construction very thoroughly and transparently. (Germany)

Difficulties and methodological problems
As the scenario method that presented by Max-Goote Expert Center is a projective one and at the same time a systematic way of Strategic thinking, it was very difficult for many Greek Experts to distinguish it from a pure scientific and predictable way of thinking.

This confusion caused some problems of misunderstanding:
1 Most experts were looking at the different scenarios as willing or unwilling future conditions. So they were mainly looking at the different strategies as measures for avoiding the one or the other situation and not as also a way of maximizing the possible positive points of the alternative futures.
2 It was very difficult for most experts and policy makers to interpret the alternative scenarios as a presentation of different future situation for strategic thinking instead of differentiated predictions.

The correlation of the different strategies to the different scenarios were weak as the experts were thinking and talking about the different policy measures having in mind 'their own scenario on the operational use of the scenario project', and were reacting according to their own 'future prediction'. (Greece)

De-institutionalisation of strategic conversation methods
Finally the project produced interesting paradox 'side-insights': joined strategic conversation is a difficult issue Germany, not least because of the fact that there is indeed already an institutionalised place of strategic conversation, namely the de-scribed 'expert-system'. This, however, also comprises quite highly institutionalised internal boundaries of established strategic conversation milieus. Issues such as global mega-trends and the demand for a stronger internationalisation also of VET-questions, might cause the overcoming of those boundaries in the long-term. (Germany)

7.4.3. Adapting the methodology
Adapte la méthodologie au contexte particulier
- Les circonstances particulières nous ont amené à nous éloigner de la méthode préconisé et de mettre en œuvre une démarche qualitative et partici-pative qui a impliqué un nombre important d'experts pendant les différentes phases.
- Néanmoins, nous utilisons la méthode originelle dans d'autres cas, notamment, dans le cadre de projets de restructuration.
- Le fait d'avoir impliqué à de nombreuses reprises des experts dans nos travaux va, en plus du processus de dissémination engagé sur base doc-

umentaire, probablement favoriser la diffusion des résultats de cette recherche, de même que la crédibilité des résultats fournis.
- Le fait de pouvoir adapter la méthodologie au contexte particulier ... (Luxembourg/Belgium)

Deepening analysis
We have also begun the process of deepening the scenarios analysis, by identifying key players in specific scenario/strategy combinations, and by starting to identify more detailed actions in relation to specific strategies. Several groups of policy makers and researchers in the UK are convinced that the scenarios method can play a useful role in helping to develop coherent and longer-term strategic approaches to training policy, and at a number of different levels. (United Kingdom)

Sustain innovation
The process that we have been engaged in has been experimental, and we think that the methodology that is developing is capable of helping to guide and sustain innovation. It has engaged the researchers and policy makers we have worked with. Forecasting and managing incremental change tend to take the relative certainties of the near future into account; scenarios thinking deals quite deliberately with uncertain processes and outcomes. Scenarios or futures work, in our view, is not the tool, but in some circumstances it will be a useful tool. (United Kingdom)

7.5. European level experience

Learning process for participants
- The method with enormous potential, however in the case of VET it still needs some adjustments in order to produce more concrete results.
- Experience of the project shows that its initial assumptions were too ambitious; especially the scope of the first stage should have been focused more on issues dealing directly with VET development. The results of this stage especially scenarios were too general to be an effective tool for decision making processes.
- The project was no doubt very valuable experience and learning process for its participants;
- I am afraid that without any follow-up the impact of the project may be very limited (Poland)

Players at the European level
- We think it has enormous potential. It is capable of adaptation so that it can be useful in a wide range of settings.
- We are using variants of the methodology in other work: notably in a project on developing strategies for the national curriculum and assessment systems in England, and in identifying training needs (Barcelona, may develop into a Barcelona/London Project.
- Linking with the other European teams has been particularly interesting and a major learning experience. The methodology should now be used to explore the strategic role in training of players at the European level, in the light of EU employment, inclusion and lifelong learning policies.
- As we have indicated, we would like to contribute to the development of a manual - something like the hitchhikers guide to scenario and strategy building.
- I'm seeing a problem locating the purpose of the first national seminar, I'm also wanting to locate a purpose for our national steering group (United Kingdom)

7.6. Strengths and weaknesses

As every research method, scenario planning has its strengths and weaknesses. Below we will describe the most important ones.

7.6.1. Strengths

Unlike traditional forecasting or market research, scenarios present alternative images instead of extrapolating current trends from the present. Scenarios also embrace qualitative perspectives and the potential for sharp discontinuities that econometric models exclude. Consequently, creating scenarios requires policy makers and managers to question their broadest assumptions about the way that the world works, so they can anticipate decisions that might be missed or denied. Within the organisation or system they are developed, scenarios provide a common vocabulary and an effective basis for communicating complex, sometimes paradoxical conditions and options.

Good scenarios are plausible and surprising; they have the power to break old stereotypes. Developing and using scenarios is rehearsing the future, and by recognising the warning signs one can avoid surprises, adapt and act effectively. Decisions that have been discussed against a range of what the future may bring are more likely to stand the test of time, produce robust and resilient strategies, and create distinct competitive advantage. Ultimately, the end result of scenario planning is not a more accurate picture of tomorrow but better decisions today (GBN, web page).

The Conference Board Europe held a small survey on scenario planning among its members (Ringland, p.34). The scenarios that they developed were mostly intended to help with investment management, but that did not turn out to be the main benefit. It was the changes in awareness, which was seen as the main benefit.

Foresight pushes the boundaries of perception in at least four major ways by:
- Consequence Assessment: assessing the implications of present actions, decisions etc.
- Early warning and guidance: detecting and avoiding problems before they occur;
- Pro-active strategy formulation: considering the present implications of possible future events;
- Normative Scenarios: envisioning aspects of possible or desired futures.
(Slaughter 1996, in Ringland, p.47)

David Mercer states the advantages of scenario construction as follows: 'Clearly, the most important outcomes are the identification of the alternative futures (and facing up to the uncertainty these imply) and developing the robust strategies to address these (as a complement to the optimal short-term strategies).' Besides that, he mentions the value of the communication process itself. The process of scenario construction consolidates relationships between participants from different parts of the organisation or the 'system'. The underlying tensions can be surfaced and positively addressed (David Mercer, homepage).

Another strength is that the scenario planning process makes uncertainties explicit. It could bring about a feeling of daring and is motivating to face the future and its uncertainties. Starting with fear for the future is turned around to positively ad-dressing the uncertainties that lie ahead.

7.6.2. Weaknesses

Because of the imaginary/creative nature of scenario planning it is essential that the participants in the process are aware of certain pitfalls when creating and implementing the scenarios and strategies.

One commonly known problem when constructing scenarios is the tension between the concept of creativity and policy innovation on the one hand and the sense of reality and connection with prevailing developments and policies on the other hand. This tension manifests itself in the relation between the three parties involved in the process, all having different frames of reference and interests: the researcher, the scenario builder and the user of the scenario. The relation between these three could be compared with that of a brick manufacturer, an architect and the client. The brick manufacturer will be concerned with the quality and characteristics of the stones that are needed in the construction. He will want to advise the architect as thoroughly as possible about the different possibilities of the material. The architect, however, seems to be more concerned with the overall perception, the harmony and unity of what is being build. And finally the client also has his own perception on the process, mostly expressed in concerns about the direct use of the construction and the related costs.

Not surprisingly the researcher, scenario builder and client often experience difficulty in communicating about the purpose and procedure of constructing scenarios. It is therefore essential that all participants are clear about the data and techniques used for the building, about the clarity of its purpose, the usefulness in the here and now and the relation of costs and benefits.

The most important and most difficult part of scenario planning is letting go of the official future. What happens is that there is often too little wild thinking, i.e. coming up with countervailing ideas. Existing ideas and policies are too much legitimised. Even when the scenarios are already constructed, there is sometimes a tendency to validate the conclusions from documentary evidence. On the other hand, scenario planning can cause too wild, futuristic thinking. Trends tend to get too far from reality, which produces scenarios without any implications. Usually this happens when making the current developments the absolute truth and ignoring current problems or undesirable trends.

One major issue when constructing scenarios is the danger that people want to add values to scenarios. They want to classify the scenarios into good/bad, desirable/undesirable, most of the time in order to be able to choose. We have already discussed that scenario planning is not about choosing the right one, just like it is not about choosing the best or most desirable. Van der Heijden (p.198, 207) writes that all scenarios should reflect worlds in which the user could live and be prepared for. Only plausibility and internal consistency should be the yardstick.

Closely related to the issue of wanting to add values to scenarios, is the general and very common idea of wanting to assign probabilities to the scenarios. Pierre (1985) gives many reasons why probability is not the question to ask of your scenarios. He states that the point, is not so much to have one scenario that 'gets it right' as to have a set of scenarios that illuminates the major forces driving the system, their interrelationships, and the critical uncertainties. It is a general tendency for people to focus on the 'as usual' scenario, since it reflects conventional wisdom. In the same way people like to pick the middle scenario as the most likely, a tendency that can easily be avoided by working with an even number of scenarios.

One other weakness of scenario planning presents itself at the stage of implementation. The best known reason for scenario planning to fail is because the scenarios are not integrated into the process and culture of the organisation. To work with scenarios it requires a certain state of mind and agreement on all the issues discussed above. This is difficult to achieve, and sometimes it needs some time and a lot of practice.

8. Annex I

8.1. Overview of 'national' scenarios and strategies

8.1.1. Austria

8.1.1.1. Scenario I – Internationalisation

DESCRIPTORS	QUANTITATIVE DESCRIPTION (¹)	QUALITATIVE DESCRIPTION
Context: Economy		
Restructuring	5	Technological change shows a strong, enduring effect and changes economic structures, methods of work, etc. Social power structures shift (for ex. reduced importance of trade unions, social partners) toward stronger individuality.
Growth	4	The focusing of competences contributes to a strong economic growth.
Competition	5	Innovation for the retention and expansion of competitiveness are for ex. strategic partnerships, mergers of international companies amongst others.
Privatisation	5	The state withdraws for the most part and creates extensive freedom through reduction of legal framework pre-requesists to a minimum (for ex. liberalisation of business hours).
Context: Labour market and social dimension		
Flexibility/ mobility	5	The labour force is mobile and flexible, whereby flexibility and mobility, especially in the upper and lower quarters of the employment levels, is very strongly pronounced.

(¹) For the quantitative description a 5 point scale was used: 1 = very little/few ... to 5 = very many/much ... The scores can vary between 1 and 5.

Work/training patterns		Economy and market determine the speed and direction of the (necessary) developments.
Inequality/ exclusion	5	Strong deregulation tendencies and technical-economic developments polarise the workforce. The need for lower qualified labourers and workmen climbs. Social security is the responsibility of the individual. The state social network limits itself to a minimum.
Organisation of work		The business processes are characterised by strong service-orientation. Work is organised in a highly flexible way, especially for qualified jobs.
Context: Demand for training		
General skills levels	3	The state offers basic training (basic skills) which can be enhanced and expanded by the individual by his/her own initiative. in addition to state structures abroad national and international private education market exists, served by ICT.
In-company provision	3	Companies take-over education tasks in order to have an influence on the type and quality of the qualifications of their employees.
Investment in training	5	VET is the task and responsibility of the individual. Personal resources/financial situation, social capital etc.) have a strong determination for the access to education.
Lifelong learning	5	VET is an integrated component of life and a determinant for vocational success.

8.1.1.2. Scenario II – Harmonisation

DESCRIPTORS	QUANTITATIVE DESCRIPTION	QUALITATIVE DESCRIPTION
Context: Economy		
Restructuring	3-4	Structural changes bring, as result, strong adaptations and diverse changes. The social proportions shift a little, or that is to say, not at all, through cushioning by the social partners. The role of the social partners will be newly defined. Alongside partially massive structural changes, proven traditions continue to exist. Modernisation is defined as the continuation of proven practices while at the same time, improvements of weak points, for ex. through technical innovations.
Growth	4	National and international cooperation have shown to be advantageous for the economic growth.
Competition		
Privatisation	3	The state creates an equalisation between liberalisation and regulation. The public sector loses a significance, but remains however, an important employer.
Context: Labour market and social dimension		
Flexibility/ mobility	3-4	Mobility and flexibility on manpower are differently pronounced. There is a need, and possibilities exist, for mobile, flexible and traditional labour models. mobility and flexibility is especially present in upper qualification levels.
Work/training patterns		

Inequality/ exclusion	3	State precautions allow deregulation to a certain degree, whereby the work force is of course polarised, although social differenced do not take the over-hand. Social security remains one of the primary tasks of the state, can however, be augmented by individual precautions (possibly supported by tax reductions).
Organisation of work		See Flexibility/mobility
Context: Demand for training		
General skills levels	4-5	The state ensures the provision of primary education with a focus on generalisable, fundamental, basic knowledge. A second (partially) legal string of private education offerers make points by providing specialised and vocationally oriented training programmes.
In-company provision	2	The state endeavours to react to the needs of business through its flexibility, but still lags behind the current trends. In-company training occurs more frequently.
Investment in training	3	The state retains an important role in the field of VET. Alongside traditional education routes, new routes of VET especially of an informal nature develop. Individuals need to invest in their VET especially for obtaining qualified, high-level jobs.
Lifelong learning	5	Lifelong learning is required for a stable and successful career.

8.1.1.3. Scenario III – Regionalisation

DESCRIPTORS	QUANTITATIVE DESCRIPTION	QUALITATIVE DESCRIPTION
Context: Economy		
Restructuring	3-4	The state takes over a central role in the relationship to internationalisation and globalisation. National markets are protected through the corresponding laws and internationalisation is made more difficult. Technological innovations make new methods of work and labour possible, which lead to comprehensive restructuring.
Growth	3-4	The protection of national markets etc. contributes to a stable, positive economic growth.
Competition	3	Innovations happen especially within the framework of national cooperations and partially through strategic international partnerships, since Austrian markets can only be cultivated by Austrian partners. Niche products and specialisation create competitive advantages that are supported by the state through legal frameworks and financial incentives.
Privatisation	2	Conditional inequalities are compensated for by state (counter) measures. Privatisation continues although state regulations remain strong.
Context: Labour market and social dimension		
Flexibility/ mobility	2-3	Mobility is of little importance. The need for labour will be primarily covered by national supply. State internal flexible structures exist regarding working hours etc.
Work/training patterns		

Inequality/ exclusion	1-2	Modernisation processes will be cushioned by corresponding legal precautions. Companies and the state divide the responsibility for social fairness.
Organisation of work		The state encourages federalism and the solidarity principle. The protection on national and regional markets receives a large importance. (see also Flexibility/mobility)
Context: Demand for training		
General skills levels	5	The state guarantees a solid basic education with a focus on general knowledge and transferable abilities and talents (e.g. learning to learn, working with new ICT etc.).
In-company provision	4-5	Companies have, due to the limited availability of human resources a strong interest in qualification and continuing education of employees. Education is task of the state, job-specific qualifications and continuing education is primarily taken over by companies. Corresponding subsidies and financial support form an incentive for companies to engage themselves.
Investment in training	3	The state provides framework conditions (for ex. quality standards) for VET. The execution happens in the majority of cases by very few private offerers with strong regional focal points. Education has a high value in society and experiences state financial support. State measures compensate for social justice.
Lifelong learning	5	LLL is important and strongly supported by the state (see also In-company provision and Investment in training).

8.1.2. Czech Republic

8.1.2.1. *Scenario I – Scepticism to changes*

DESCRIPTORS	QUANTITATIVE DESCRIPTION	QUALITATIVE DESCRIPTION
Context: Economic dimensions		
Restructuring		Restructuring in the economy occurs under strong influence of individual state interventions. In the industry still dominate large companies with government support effected by power groups. The government regulates as public so private sector by chaotic intervention policy. Some sectors and power groups and some sectoral MSE are supported. Some business companies are still in common ownership with the state and are politically effected.
Growth		Middle- to long-term stagnation to decline in economy growth. Non-predicted inflation development. Labour productivity stagnation. Real wages growth stagnation. No improvement in regional disparities neither in unemployment rate nor in GDP per inhabitant, in spite of expended public budgets resources. Long-term unemployment becomes unsettled problem. Social partnership is strongly effected by government changes after each general election and its results are not helpful for social stability. The influence of government is high. The emphasis is put on social and public aspects of economic policy, though based on high public expenditures. The partnership approach emphases the labour stability without social shocks. Co-operation between large enterprises and the government gives priority to some power groups. Shareholders interests are effected by lobbying.
Competition		In spite of strong government interventions and regulations the competitiveness at the labour market stagnates. Quite low competitiveness towards foreign market. Stagnation of knowledge-based sectors rate in production and

	employment context. Information technologies play a significant role in development of the economy. ICT effect the economy. ICT can be a factor deepening social inequations.
Privatisation	Privatisation has stopped and does not continue. Government ownership in economic sector is still significant and politically effected. Prevails the contribution of private sector in GNP generating.
Demand for lower/mediate skills manual ones	Companies forecast their own needs in skills and qualified workers but traditional professions continue to be supported. Market demand for low-skilled workers decreases. There are gaps in skills at all education levels. There is an excess of some professions, namely.
Context: Social-labour dimensions	
Flexibility/ mobility	Labour flexibility level follows the qualification level. Labour mobility level is quite high but in employment context affected by unstable situation in business sphere. There is an unbalance between work and education resulted from inadequate approach of enterprises to human resource development.
Work training patterns	Thanks to governmental subsidies big companies not doing well survive with the present distribution of work and workload. At the same time minor companies, first of all in the sector of services are thriving and in a small scale companies with foreign capital where economic and commercial dimensions in workload of staff are more and more predominating, coping with problem situations off routine activities, work with information, interpersonal communication. The number of people employed in 'underground economy' increases, people with quality education try to find a job abroad on a large scale. In continuing education selected well doing companies organise courses for their employees (rather for their management).

Inequalities	Hardly ensured social steadiness at the high cost of public budgets resources. Unemployment among socially non-adaptable and elder people is a big problem. Systemless and ad hoc solutions prevail in the active employment policy. Inequity in incomes stagnates under conditions of wages growth stagnation. Difficult access to employment for low-skilled people. The social allowances at the margin of public budget resources acceptability.
Organisation of labour	In many companies prevails traditional practice and hierarchical organisation structure. Employing the people from abroad is regulated by governmental regulations. Information technologies play a significant role in labour organisation in business sphere and a great deal of employees use PC and mobile phone. Negligent deal of distance working employees. The importance of social skills grows up together with hierarchic level of working functions. General industrial and local common bargaining based on partnership exists but works rather formally. The social partnership (tripartite) is initiated by trade unions. The key partner promoting the equality of opportunities and requiring the social exclusion improving are trade unions. Trade unions are very active, strikes affect economy.
Context: Training dimensions	
General skills	In initial VET prevail training in public and governmental institutions but additional VET is partly developed as in public so in private institutions. VET providers flexibility in accordance with demand from institutions and individual part is limited. Priority for VET governmental programmes are groups at risk, elder people and unemployed. VET is targeted to help individuals to settle the need to change their skills. Individuals finance contribution in skills growth is rather smaller. The initial VET is funded or supported from public resources in accordance with the national programme. The cultural context of the education is not specifically formulated.

In-company training	VET is provided based on partnership with prevailing role of the government. The content of qualifications and curriculum slightly react to company specific needs and labour market needs. A great deal of VET is provided by public institutions. Programmes for groups at risk are provided by government supported agencies and by government. Employers and their trade unions organise the training programmes only in minimum extent in their own facilities. Under subsidiarity a lot of decisions are left at regional, local or sectoral level but with strong governmental co-ordination. Governmental supporting programmes are organized for specific target groups. New forms of training and education are developed only a little.
Willingness to invest	Prevail public initial VET, while training in flexible skills and short-time courses is less frequent, with participation of business sector. The range and number of public schools stagnate after the initial development. The willingness of companies to invest in their employees training is conditioned by the level of co-funding from public resources. There is expected the high contribution of individuals in funding their qualification improvement.
Life long learning	Though the VET is declared to be life long but as business sector so individuals neglect it. The priority is given to initial VET, the additional VET does not develop any system and is quite neglected. Generally, there can be no co-ordination. ICT is insufficiently represented because of limited funding possibilities from public resources. Out of school it fully depends on economic level of the family

8.1.2.2. Scenario II – Growth – Solidarity

DESCRIPTORS	QUANTITATIVE DESCRIPTION	QUALITATIVE DESCRIPTION
Context: Economic dimensions		
Restructuring		Restructuring in the economy occurs under state interference into market processes. The government effect on restructuring. Supranational companies settled in the country sustain their supply basis of Czech companies. Establishment, development and failure of large and small companies in some sectors are a general feature. Government regulates as public so private sector through intervention policy. Different sectors and power groups (even in regional context) are supported by indirect mechanisms. There are large business companies with significant share of managerial and employee shares or fully owned by management and employees.
Growth		Moderate economic growth approximates to the growth level in advanced EU countries. Relatively low inflation rate. Productivity of work approximating to (or comparable with) advanced countries. Moderate growth in real wages. Moderate improvement of regional disparities in unemployment rate and GNP per inhabitant but that do not correspond with resources expended from public budget. Long-term unemployment will be mitigated through social programmes (EU influence). The emphasis is put on social and public context of the economic policy including development of the solid infrastructure and high quality services. Partnership approach emphasises the stability of work without social shocks, equal opportunities and fight against exclusion of special groups. General industrial and local common bargaining. Shareholders interests are balanced with those of social partners.

Competition	Competitiveness at the market is achieved through co-operation between more partners or stakeholders. National and international capital will follow incentives provided in considerable extent and work force value. Differences in regions will increase, regions and sectors with developed technologies and foreign investments will be competitive. Moderate growth of knowledge-based sectors in production and employment context. Information technologies play a significant role in development of the economy. ICT will significantly effect the world economy. ICT can be a factor deepening social inequations.
Privatisation	Quite high privatisation rate in the economy. Government ownership share in economic sector is going down. Prevails the private sector contribution in GNP generating.
Demand for lower/mediate skills manual ones	Monitoring and forecasting needs in skills and qualified workers is a part of discussion with social partners. Market demand for low-skilled workers is decreasing and is differentiated in accordance with the economic development of the region. There are gaps in qualifications namely in the highest degree. There is an excess of some professions, namely manual ones.
Context: Social-labour dimensions	
Flexibility/ mobility	The workforce flexibility rate grows up parallel with the level of qualification. Partnership approach stresses the stability of work, level of workforce mobility differentiates. Centralised mechanisms are used for forecasting and meeting needs in qualification. This provides the basis for the balance between the work and education, in spite of disparities existing at some professions.

Work training patterns	Thanks to governmental subsidies big companies not doing well survive with the present distribution of work and workload. At the same time minor companies , first of all in the sector of services are thriving as well as companies with foreign capital where economic and commercial dimensions in workload of staff is predominating, coping with problem situations off routine activities, work with information , interpersonal communication, in the case of foreign investors communication in foreign language, modern optimalisation methods are applied in management, integration and interconnection of activities take place. Planning and at the same time checking activities predominate. The number of people employed in government administration increases; people with quality education try to find a job abroad. State-aided courses predominate in continuing education , distance education is being developed.
Inequalities	Social steadiness is ensured at the high cost of public budgets resources. Unemployment among socially non-adaptable and elder people remains to be a problem. The active employment policy reacts to regional and sectoral disparities. Inequity in incomes is still in acceptable limits at the cost of wages growth stagnation. Difficult access to employment for low-skilled people. 'Generous' social allowances demanding public budget resources.
Organisation of labour	The government supports the change in work organisation. Tendency towards reducing the size of enterprises and their higher flexibility. Employing workers from abroad is regulated by governmental regulations. Information technologies play an important role in work organisation in business sphere and a great deal of employees use PC and mobile phone. A moderate growth in distance working

employees rate. The importance level of social skills grows up parallel with hierarchical level of working functions. General industrial and local common bargaining based on partnership. The government initiates the social partnership and the economic policy is agreed based on consent. The government is a key partner promoting the equality of opportunities and improving the social exclusion. Trade unions belong among social partners and contribute in social peace.

Context:
Training dimensions

General skills

In addition to governmental programmes there are also very important the enterprise and private VET. VET(public sector parallel with the private and nongovernmental sectors) is targeted to assist individuals to meet the need to change skills. Not only key skills but also namely managerial and ICT skills are very significant. In governmental VET programmes the priority is given to groups at risk, elder people and unemployed. VET is targeted to help the individuals to meet the need to change skills. The priority is the inclusion of all social groups into training process. Individuals adequately contribute in funding the qualification improvement but their contribution is quite low. Initial and further VET is funded or supported from public sources with the certain co-participation of individuals/companies. Cultural context of the training is oriented towards education for citizenship in regional, national and European context. Prevails public training. Providers of additional VET are flexible to reflect both, demand in form of public orders and labour market impulses. Responsibility for preparation and larger VET flexibility is shifted to regions or sectors effecting by central mechanisms.

In-company training	VET is provided based on partnership under balanced market and institutional approaches. An effort is put to harmonise qualification with labour market needs. The government encourages the contribution of companies in training and at the same time there exist a competition represented by business companies. Prevail training institutions supported by government, however, there is a competition represented by business companies. Agencies supported by government introduce changes in qualification, funding and organisation of VET programmes after discussion with social partners. Under subsidiarity are many decisions left on regional, local or sectoral level but with central co-ordination. The training is shifted from 'off the job' to 'on the job' training. 'On the job' training and distance and Internet training are applied.
Willingness to invest	Prevail public education and training in initial VET, in flexible skills innovations, short-time courses and higher education. Private education and training institutions present some counterbalance for public school system. The willingness of companies to invest in their employees training is differentiated and reflects the quality of motivation mechanisms.
Life long learning	Though the VET is declared to be life long so, thanks to soft social environment, is this principle accepted only in some professions. Additional VET is generating as additional following system. Co-ordination needs are very high, namely in interconnecting certificates and in developing a functional information system. ICT is developed adequately to possibilities given by funding from public resources. Step by step it gains its importance as a tool of non-formal education. Labour mobility liberates and common acceptation of qualifications becomes more general.

8.1.2.3. Scenario III – Growth – Competitiveness

DESCRIPTORS	QUANTITATIVE DESCRIPTION	QUALITATIVE DESCRIPTION
Context: Economic dimensions		
Restructuring		Restructuring in the economy occurs under natural market processes. Establishment, development and failure of large and small companies in some sectors is a general feature. Supranational companies settled in the country sustain their supply basis of Czech companies. Minimum government interventions into economic processes, governmental policy aiming at environment creation. Small- and middle-sized companies preserve in many sectors only with difficulty. Management in the most business companies has no ownership relations to the company.
Growth		Economic growth accelerating with the higher growth rate (over the growth level in EU countries). Reasonable inflation rate, work productivity comparable with developed countries. Real wages increasing in association with economic growth. Non-dramatic regional disparities. Long-time unemployment remains to be a problem at groups at risk. In economic development are the most important interests of companies and stakeholders including lower importance of collective agreements. Intensity rate of co-operation between public and private organisations is low. Partners are directly responsible for selected types of education and training. Shareholders interests are strong and oriented rather in short-time perspective.

Competition	Competitiveness at the market is generating and accelerating by market mechanism. National and international capital follows incentives provided and work force value. Differences in regions are increasing, regions and sectors with developed technologies and foreign investments are able to be competitive. Acceleration rate of knowledge-based sectors in production and employment context. Information technologies play a significant role in development of the economy. ICT development is essential and aims at the total penetration into the economy.
Privatisation	The high privatisation rate includes also the net sectors. Government ownership share in economic sector is minimum and negligent.
Demand for lower/mediate skills manual ones	Demand and supply of skills is generally effected by market signals. Market demand for low and middle-qualified work force goes down. The demand for the highest education degree, or qualification/skills is modestly higher than supply. There is excess of some professions, namely manual ones.
Context: Social-labour dimensions	
Flexibility/ mobility	Workforce flexibility level increases and grows up by the qualification level. Workforce mobility level is differentiated. The high mobility is only among workers with the highest qualification who are seeking the high remuneration for work. There is unbalance between work and education, but shows the tendency for improvement.
Work training patterns	Companies, which are not doing well, are liquidated, the quantity of employees is replaced by their quality, the scope and the level of qualification is decisive. Economic and commercial dimensions, coping with problems off routine activities, work with information, interpersonal communication including communication in foreign language predominates., integration and interconnection of

	activities take place. The number of people working at home (it is conditioned by generally expansion and availability of internet), as well as the numbers of people employed with more employers, part time employed and self employed people are going up. The need of people adaptable to changes in workload is increasing and it requires the necessity of further education which can very often have a form of self-education - starting with training on-the job and ending with education based on using ITK technology (multi medial education organised as distance education), education is a significant tool of labour force mobility (study visits abroad).
Inequalities	There is affected social steadiness. Among socially non-adaptable and elderly is higher unemployment rate. The active employment policy is focused on socially excluded groups of people. Increasing inequality in incomes within the general wages increasing. Difficult access to job for low educated people. Small social support provided by employer or government.
Organisation of labour	Speed changes in organisation structure of enterprises with the aim to achieve rather short-time results (profits) and profitability. Employing the people from abroad in business sector is subjected to principles of market balance and market signals about wages value. Control mechanisms are indirect. Information technologies play an important role in work organisation in business sector. There accelerates the distance working employees rate but is not yet very significant. The significance of social skills grows up by the hierarchic level of work functions. The government plays secondary role in relations between employees and employers. Social partnership or tripartite shifted from the national level to the regional level. Trade unions are very active but their work looks to be rather uncontrolled.

Context: Training dimensions		
General skills		The government regulates only basic national standards. Training, namely additional VET, is in a large extent, provided by private bodies. Together with key skills there are important namely managerial and ICT skills. Non-formal training is officially certificated. The social tension generates need for training and VET for elder people, young people at risk, unemployed, etc. but this is not the key priority. Individuals are expected to invest themselves in their training and education as they consider it to be an investment with very high rate of return. Individuals choose themselves the training institutions and content of qualification. Cultural context of education is not prior, the priority is to make use of the qualification and education at the labour market. There is free competition between training institutions across the private/public sector. VET providers are flexible and follow market signals and demand from the side of private and public sectors and individuals. Responsibility for preparation and larger VET flexibility is shifted to regions or sectors and there preserve requirements of national curriculum.
	In-company training	VET, namely additional VET, reflect namely labour market needs. The content of qualifications and curriculum is defined by employers. Economically strong companies provide training programmes and programmes for additional VET. Business training programmes and VET programmes providers are mostly private agencies. Qualifications and VET programmes are defined based on significant labour market signals. Curriculum and certificates in VET are split in smaller and smaller modules and the content differs sector by sector and situation by situation. The training is shifted from 'off the job' to training 'on the job'. There is a great deal of training 'on the job', distance and an Internet training.

Willingness to invest	Generally, the individual (consumer) chooses qualification, training institution and a VET form. Learners have an option to choose public VET or private one. Private schools form by its range and number a significant counterbalance to public school system. The willingness of the companies to invest in the training of their employees is large and is associated with expectation of higher competitiveness. Private individuals are motivated to invest in training as they expect of it a high rate of return.
Life long learning	Additional VET is the basic condition for worker to gain his place in market environment. The additional VET is the priority for strategically thinking companies. The initial VET is taken as a basis for additional necessary VET taking fast innovation into account. In co-ordination context there is put an emphasis on solid information system and on interconnection of both VET areas. ICT is of essential importance, pervades through the training content and is an essential part of training programmes (tool) and an essential part of the content. It is the necessary condition for distance training.

8.1.3. Estonia

8.1.3.1. Scenario I – Good Start

General description of scenario		Limited restructuring + public sector intervention at the initial level
European processes		EU accession delayed, uncertain, many obstructions to movement of labour even after accession. Baltic Sea region is relatively peripheral in world economy

DESCRIPTORS	QUANTITATIVE DESCRIPTION	QUALITATIVE DESCRIPTION
Context: Economy		
Technological restructuring and modernisation of economy and companies	2	Very moderate/limited Technological restructuring concerns very limited share of irms. R&D activity is considerable in the case of very limited number of big enterprises, especially those, controlled by foreign capital.
Economic space		Northern & Western Europe, primarily Scandinavia and Baltic states, Germany and some other.
Economic growth		Low- 3-4% as annual average. Relatively few investments, mainly money from Nordic-based main offices. Leading sectors: trade, tourism, personal services, food, timber, assembly and subcontract works.
Models of competition (importexport)		Cheap production input (cheap local labour, low-value raw material, cheap services).
Demand for low and medium-level labour		High, economy absorbs mainly work force with low and medium level skills.

Context:
Labour market (and developments of social dimension)

Flexibility and mobility of labour	3	Moderate, risk groups will have better training and possibilities in the labour market.
Work-related training models	2	Very limited, primarily connected to concrete changes in technology at the company level.
Inequality	3	Living standard is generally low, services relatively expensive. Inequality is on the average or relatively low level because of public support to certain risk groups (youth).

Context:
Training/vocational education (demand side, i.e. demand):

For general skills	4	High.
Training at work	2	Weakly developed. Based on the introduction of new technology.
(Private sectors) desire to invest (in training)	2	Low.
Life-long leaning (motivation for learning increases among the elderly according to change of employment models (age prospects?)	3	Based on strong primary-level education; but controlled by market forces and depends on opportunities.
Partnership model		Dual system at initial level of VET, realised by the regional VET centres and vocational councils.

8.1.3.2. Scenario II – Splitting into Two

General description of scenario		*Strong restructuring + liberal development*
European processes		*Joining to EU (as an diverse unit) takes place. There are many obstructions to movement of labour even after accession,* *Baltic Rim economic space is developing and dynamic*

DESCRIPTORS	**QUANTITATIVE DESCRIPTION**	**QUALITATIVE DESCRIPTION**
Context: Economy		
Technological restructuring and modernisation of economy and companies	4	Uneven, split in two Highly different level of restructuring in different sectors of economy and regions. Tallinn-Helsinki integration is stronger than Tallinn integration with rest of Estonia.
Economic space		Global, both West- and East-directed economic relations are important.
Economic growth		Relatively high, 5-6% as annual average, but unstable and uneven (some sectors will modernise significantly, some not) Leading sectors: trade, transit, tourism, business and information services, IKT-based services and industry (as subcontracting sector mainly).
Models of competition (import-export)		Different according to sectors of economy: cheap services (tourism) in the domestic and knowledge in the international sector.
Demand for low and medium-level labour		Uneven, relatively low in advanced sectors and technologically advanced and IT-based service sector companies, relatively high in some sectors and SMEs.

Context: **Labour market (and developments of social dimension)**		
Flexibility and mobility of labour	4	High, especially in the case of some labour market segments.
Work-related training models	3	In rapidly developing sectors inevitable, controlled and initiated by parent firms.
Inequality	5	Inequality level is very high - polarisation trends are prevailing. Employment will polarise as well by sectors and by regions.
Context: **Training/vocational education (demand side, i.e. demand)**		
For general skills	4-5	High.
Training at work	3	Highly developed in some sectors.
(Private sectors) desire to invest (in training)	3-5	High; private sector.
Life-long leaning (motivation for learning increases among the elderly according to change of employment models (age prospects?)	4	Opportunities differ in various sectors in an considerable extent.
Partnership model		Sector-based partnership model, realised by sector organisations or by corporation.

8.1.3.3. Scenario III – Dissolving

General description of scenario		Strong restructuring + public sector intervention at the innovation systems level
European processes		Joining to EU (as an integrated unit) has taken place. EU supports education and innovation via various programmes. Free movement of labour. Baltic Sea economic space is developing and dynamic

DESCRIPTORS	QUANTITATIVE DESCRIPTION	QUALITATIVE DESCRIPTION
Context: Economy		
Technological restructuring and modernisation of economy and companies	4	Strong restructuring Economy will highly open, innovative, and mobile. The restructuring processes concerns almost all sectors of economy.
Economic space		Global, both West- and East-directed economic ties and markets are important.
Economic growth		High, 6-7% as annual average. many international investments and capital (foothold for entering Eastern markets). Leading sectors: transit, trade, tourism and business services, IT, engineering. Timber & furniture, food and some other traditional industries (metal) will completely restructure.
Models of competition (import-export)		Knowledge-based products and services dominating.
Demand for low and medium-level labour		Low. The number of skilled workers´ level jobs would diminish and split into two: some of them will belong to the technician-level jobs, some of them to the blue-collars of IT industry.

Context: Labour market (and developments of social dimension)		
Flexibility and mobility of labour	5	Extremely high, due to the continuing changes.
Work-related training models	4	Varied.
Inequality	4	Relatively high especially because of continues rapid structural changes in the labour market Unemployment will become a problem for most risk groups (people lagging behind). In the same time there is lack of certain highly qualified professionals in certain fields (science and technology).
Context: Training/vocational education (demand side, i.e. demand)		
For general skills	5	High.
Training at work	4-5	Highly developed, new concepts have been introduced.
(Private sectors) desire to invest (in training)	4	High.
Life-long leaning (motivation for learning increases among the elderly according to change of employment models (age prospects?)	5	Life-long learning is part of (working) life. But also depends on individual resources.
Partnership model		Corporation-centred model or regional model.

Annex I | 183

8.1.4. Greece

8.1.4.1. Scenario I – Complete Domination of the Market and Increased Inequalities on Multiple Levels

DESCRIPTORS	QUANTITATIVE DESCRIPTION	QUALITATIVE DESCRIPTION
Context: Economy		
Restructuring	5	The process of restructuring the economy is going ahead without the implementation of integrated development policies. The harmonious functioning of markets, in conditions of great or complete liberalisation, is considered as a basic regulatory factor in the sphere of the economy, thus isolating the 'social' sphere and the sphere of international relations, as basic fields which equally help address the impacts of the changes. Policies based the economy's 'automatic' regulatory function for dealing with the effects of globalisation predominate. A result of this is the dissemination of restructuring, which leads to the concentration of production in certain areas (industries-enterprises), while other areas fall into decline. The basic structural characteristics of the country's structure (system) of production remain unchanged. Restrictions in relation to the country's productive capacity are ignored, as are those determined by international economic relations, as two basic factors determining the potential for and the rates of growth of a (small) open economy.
Growth	3	Restrictions in relation to the country's productive capacity are ignored, as are those determined by international economic relations, as two basic factors determining the potential for and the rates of growth of a (small) open economy. 'Arbitrary', selective improvement has been seen

in the competitiveness of enterprises - industries. The forces of production as a whole have no participation in this, and as a result social inequalities have intensified and problems are addressed by shifting 'burdens' onto wage costs and reduced public spending.

An important number of large enterprises are continually investing in technological modernisation, by drawing on capital via the stock market. They have penetrated external markets, particularly those of the Balkan countries, to a large extent. The installation and expansion of units of production in these countries restricts their domestic production activity exclusively to the sectors of research, development and marketing of new products.

| Competition | 5 |

Enterprises in the sectors of banking/insurance, telecommunications, information technology, chemical products, lumber/furniture and certain textile and ready-to-wear clothing industries, which are oriented towards the global market, show a high degree of specialisation and penetration of the markets of the Balkan and Mediterranean countries. Some have already become regional multinational enterprises, thus increasing the degree of dependence of the local economies. At the same time, the fact that they do not collaborate with other multinationals in their sectors results in confrontation over control of new markets.

Inside the economy, the process of mergers and acquisitions has come to an end. In the aforementioned industries, productive activity has decreased significantly, both with regard to employment and in relation to the variety of manufactured products. Employment has fallen, and several areas face acute problems of unemployment and depression of local economies. The rapid increase in imports of cheaper and better quality goods by the industries mentioned above have exacerbated the problems of small and medium-sized enterprises. A significant number of SMEs, unable to meet the demands of global competition, have already closed down. Others have survived, sustained more and more by lower labour costs. Workers' benefits are kept to a minimum and the quality of their production has suffered. In effect, they sell cheap, second-quality goods on the local market. Environmental protection specifications are systematically violated. A tiny number of SMEs function as subcontractors for the few large enclaves of the global economy. Very small family businesses face increased problems of survival. Only certain craft industries which have turned to production of 'sophisticated' products have survived. Other survivors have included small craft and trading companies producing products for personal use and consumption - which mainly target tourists and the neighbourhood economy.

The number of people employed in the agricultural sector has stopped falling, as the possibilities of finding employment in the other sectors of the economy have decreased. The increase in productivity has caused underemployment in a large number of agricultural workers. Many areas face problems of drought due to the exhaustion of aquifers. In very few areas are successful models of agro tourism and/or organic agriculture (vegetables-fruit - cotton) implemented. Most farmers sell their produce at very low prices because of imports from other countries. Small, fragmented holdings are still the norm, and the living conditions of most farmers have deteriorated. Services, tourism in particular, are the main economic activity. Some areas and islands have been transformed into resorts providing specialised, high-quality tourist services aimed at high-income customers. In the rest of the country, tour operators monopolise tourism enterprises based on the provision of cheap tourist packages. At the same time, an adherence exclusively to showcase works has degraded the built environment at large.

The business environment is not regulated as a whole (institutions, research, technological infrastructure, education-training), and there is a serious inability to develop partnerships between enterprises.

The state is unable to make overall provision for new redistribution norms, and focuses on restrictive regulations in the sector of economic policy. There is a lack of initial distribution of incomes and wealth, and the market result cannot lead to a maximisation of social well-being. Economic 'rationality' has a limited field of implementation.

The reduction of tax coefficients in the competitive enclaves of the global economy and the decrease in state revenue due to lower incomes and production restrict the state's economic potential. Services to citizens are confined to a few rudimentary benefits.

Wherever the problems are particularly sharp, the state intervenes from time to time in the capacity of fire-fighter. Without the help of the 'Cohesion Fund', infrastructure works would be restricted to infrastructure of limited scope in the 'enclaves of development'.

| Privatisation | 5 | Privatisation policies are losing any comparative advantages they may have had. The private sector becomes less and less able to intervene, state restructuring policies for modernisation of public sector enterprises decrease in relation to the possible choices for regulation (sell-off, supervision and subcontracting, capital sell-off, socialisation, operation according to private economic criteria). This results in non-competitiveness (in a totally competitive environment) and the preservation of the 'defensive' features of the public sector (more |

		employment retention, cheap provision of goods), and a serious problem of an increased public debt is created.
Demand for lower/mediate skills		The demand of skills is focusing mainly at low and mediate level and only a limited number of very large firms are demanding high level skills
Context: Employment and labour market		
Flexibility/ mobility	5	Labour occupies a lower place in the process of production. The efforts of most enterprises to sustain themselves on lower labour costs in order to meet the demands of international competition has led to a further de facto and de jure deregulation of the labour market and of labour relations. This has brought about a deterioration of the status of workers, which is expressed in lower incomes, fewer social benefits, less social protection, the proliferation of low-skilled jobs with no prospects of advancement, work intensification, a rapid increase in uninsured/undeclared jobs, various forms of seasonal, casual and part-time employment, flexible working hours, and general insecurity with regard to work. The decline of whole industries, especially in manufacturing, and the shutdown of a large number of small and medium-sized enterprises has led the phenomenon of mass unemployment to new heights, and it is made even more acute by the restriction of the public sector of the economy and the falloff in services which were associated with the welfare state.
Work training patterns	3	The composition of employment has changed significantly. The share of small enterprises, self-employed people and assisting family members in the secondary and tertiary sectors has been reduced, and the share of paid employment in the total labour force has increased. Within paid employment the confinement of

workers to the secondary sector is continuing and intensifying, and the number of workers in the tertiary sector is increasing, particularly in tourism-related sectors. However, employment in the public sector is decreasing even more. The labour market is fragmented and consists essentially of four categories of workers.

A small fraction of workers are employed in steady, well-paid jobs. They make up the core of sectors and enterprises which have completed the process of economic restructuring and are able to stand up to international competition.

A large segment consists of people working under open-ended contracts in enterprises and industries sustained by low labour costs, as well as workers with relatively steady employment in lower-ranking, lower-paid jobs in the services sector, with no prospects for professional advancement and a high rate of hiring and dismissals.

Another extensive peripheral group of workers is employed in competitive enterprises and industries as part-time or temporary staff, under 'zero-hours' contracts, in a relation of self-employment concealing subordination, etc. This group also contains workers who go in and out of the employment system under various forms of legal or undeclared/uninsured employment.

Finally, a large part of the labour force is marginalized. In a situation of long-term unemployment, this group consists of disillusioned unemployed people who are no longer in position even to look for a job. They are socially excluded, marginalized people.

Inequalities	5	Increased unemployment, uninsured work and flexible forms of employment have created serious problems for the social insurance system.

The fact that policy and the state no longer play a regulatory, interventionist role in forming social relations, and have restricted themselves to

		monitoring developments in the economy and safeguarding the conditions for functioning of the free market has led to a market economy characterised by a high level of social inequalities, since no provision has been made for all citizens to share on an equal footing, as far as possible, in social assets and social values. However, this depends on each person's skills and abilities, as well as on labour market accessibility. In this framework, exacerbated inequalities in income and phenomena of social exclusion and social decline particularly affect the more vulnerable groups of the labour force, including older workers, young people with low levels of education and immigrants.
Organisation of labour	3	High unemployment, a lower position of labour and the widespread development of flexible forms of employment have brought about a further weakening of the trade union movement, which now faces increased problems in approaching and organising broad, strongly differentiated groups of wage-earners, along with significant difficulties in bringing together and representing the interests of all these different groups. At the same time, however, the system of labour relations has become more confrontational. This is because, on the one hand, the weakened position of the trade union movement now allows the employers' side to take decisions without seeking its consent. On the other, the sharpening of the problems of poverty, downgrading of labour and social marginalisation have compelled large groups of workers to take militant action to claim basic labour and social rights.
Context: Training/Skills/Knowledge		
General Skills	5	The demand of general skills is a prerequisite for the movement of the insecure employees

In-company training	2	The number of unemployed people and workers who take part in continuing and in-company training is constantly increasing. The number of enterprises implementing and financing the training of their workers is relatively limited. The big competitive enterprises have developed their own internal structures for continuing training of workers; they are indifferent to broader national and regional policies. In addition, the desire of such enterprises to increase their investment in human resources is becoming stronger and stronger, inasmuch as it is emerging as a decisive factor in the processes of restructuring, introduction of innovations and increasing their competitive advantage. For other enterprises, staff training is not a priority, or is restricted to offering rudimentary training activities, which however fail to help boost their competitiveness.
Willingness to invest	3	Vocational training policy is designed and implemented in a fragmented fashion, due to the absence of integrated development policies. A dualism is seen in the provision of training services: On the one hand, some programmes are addressed to highly specialised staff, in order to meet the needs of enterprises and industries taking part in the processes of international competition. On the other hand, many programmes are focused on supporting unemployed people and socially excluded groups. At the same time, limited flexibility and strict standardisation of training programmes have been noted.
Life long learning	3	The involvement of institutions in the planning and implementation of training is, in a fragmented way, determined to a great degree by individual policy needs or specific needs and interests of the organisations involved, and not by an overall national policy. The lack of planning for training on the basis of a commonly accepted system of diagnosing and defining needs for occupational skills, on the local and sectoral level helps further restrict the part played by commercial training providers in standardised training processes.

Specialities are determined centrally, without following market trends and demands, and without differentiation into a regional and a local level. This vague determination of specialities results in a failure to link vocational training with the needs of the market and enterprises.

The limited flexibility of training programmes minimises their potential for reform as the content of specialities and new learning techniques evolve. Training is restricted to provision of specialised knowledge, as more measurable, whereas demand is increasing for general adaptation, communication, organisation and initiative-taking skills.

The lack of mechanisms for diagnosing needs on a regional, local and sectoral level and the limited part played by training bodies in implementing standardised programmes also restrict the role of vocational training as a means of social inclusion. The social task of training is restricted to an education grant, or alternatively other passive policies to boost employment, without guaranteeing access for broad social categories or exploiting the effectiveness of training as an active so policy measure.

Training is playing an increased role as a mechanism for social protection. The changes in the composition of the labour force with increased participation of economic immigrants have resulted in a broader range of trainees including population groups with language and cultural particularities, reinforcing the social and cultural dimension of training. Training bodies, however, do not orient their services towards the needs of enterprises, particularly SMEs. School and work remain two different worlds.

Initial training remains alienated from the needs of the labour market and no complementary relationship is formed with continuing vocational training programmes.

The recognition and certification of informal training is limited to narrow administrative and formal procedures lacking any real value.

8.1.4.2. Scenario II – 'Individual and Selective Responses to the Effects of Globalisation'

DESCRIPTORS	QUANTITATIVE DESCRIPTION	QUALITATIVE DESCRIPTION
Context: Economy		
Restructuring	4	The process of restructuring the economy has come to an end, and has had a strong, universal impact on the economy and social organisation as a whole. A basic regulatory factor in the sphere of the economy is the smooth functioning of markets, in conditions of extensive or even complete freedom. This isolates the spheres of the 'social' and of international relations, as areas of equal importance helping to address the effects of the changes. Although the restructuring is seen as a permanent, inevitable process, it is not sought for in the framework of integrated business strategies, but piecemeal. Many enterprises have introduced technological modernisation without restructuring their organisational model or training their labour force. Others implement internal flexibility (part-time and casual employment, subcontracting), but are indifferent to employment security or increased knowledge and skills for the labour force, large segments of which are underemployed. A large number of small and medium-sized enterprises implement policies regarding working time arrangements and reduction of direct and indirect wage costs, in order to meet the challenges of globalisation. The labour market is fragmented and there is a shortage of specialised manpower. The economy and organisation of production are characterised by a lack of synchronisation on many levels, which causes 'friction', conflicts and delays in meeting market demands. The results of new product research are adopted and implemented by only a small number of enterprises.

Growth	4	The growth of the economy has reached an intermediate level, but the gap between it and the more developed economies continues to exist. Selective policies of intervention in the functioning of the economy for dealing with the impacts of globalisation are the most common. The fact that sectoral policies are implemented in the banking, insurance, foodstuffs/beverages, tourism and non-metal products industries and not in other equally crucial sectors of the economy (textiles, construction, primary sector) has given rise to a dualism. The industries in the first category are integrated in the global market, but those in the second category are experiencing severe institutional and structural problems which reduce their competitiveness. This leads to a concentration of production in certain areas (industries-enterprises) and a corresponding decline in other areas. The basic structural characteristics of the country's structure (system) of production remain unchanged. Services are the predominant economic activity, and the primary sector has contracted.
Competition	4	An 'arbitrary', selective improvement in the competitiveness of enterprises-industries can be seen, without the participation of the forces of production as a whole. This has brought about increased social inequalities, and problems are dealt with through strong shifts of the 'burdens' to wage costs and restricted public spending. In order to meet the demands of competitiveness, small enterprises in particular seek to develop partnerships, networks and collaborations, but these do not produce proportionate positive results, because they comprise fragmentary policies which are outside the framework of integrated restructuring strategies.

Privatisation	4	In order to meet the demands of competitiveness, small enterprises in particular seek to develop partnerships, networks and collaborations, but these do not produce proportionate positive results, because they comprise fragmentary policies, which are outside the framework of integrated restructuring strategies.
Demand for lower/mediate skills		In order to meet the demands of competitiveness, small enterprises in particular seek to develop partnerships, networks and collaborations, but these do not produce proportionate positive results, because they comprise fragmentary policies which are outside the framework of integrated restructuring strategies.
Context: Employment and labour market		
Flexibility/ mobility	4	The place of labour in the production process is suffering the consequences of the competitiveness in the economy. With the exception of top-level, highly specialised staff in the core of modernised enterprises, the situation of other workers as regards labour relations completely deregulated (part-time, casual, seasonal employment, works contracts, 'zero-hours' contracts, etc.), and jobs are characterised by low pay, limited protection and no possibility of professional advancement. A prerequisite for the technological modernisation of enterprises is the employment of highly specialised and educated staff. A large number of workers face problems in adapting to the demands of technological changes, and are at risk for unemployment and marginalisation. Privatisations and the contraction of the welfare state limit the possibility that part of the unemployed will be absorbed by the public sector.

Work training patterns	4	The employment rate in the public sector, in agriculture and in manufacturing has fallen to a significant degree, whereas the employment rate in the non-state related services sector has risen substantially. The labour market is split into three parts: into one segment of the labour force which is in full-time, steady employment (but is highly diversified internally according to industry, enterprise and job), into a regional segment in flexible employment/underemployment, which now enjoys the protection of certain elementary workers' rights, on paper at least, since flexible forms of employment have been made official, but which is also low-paid and low-skilled and lacks prospects for professional advancement, and into a marginalized segment consisting of long-term unemployed and various groups suffering from social exclusion.
Inequalities	4	The increase in unemployment and in flexible forms of employment has created serious problems for the system of social insurance. Pushing the 'social issue' aside has led to a sharpening of social inequalities. One segment of the population including shareholders and executives in modern, competitive enterprises, people in show business, etc. enjoys an ever higher proportion of total income. At the other extreme, the poor segment is expanding; it includes workers in low-level jobs, who are underemployed, unemployed or retired, and marginalized groups of the population.
Organisation of labour	4	One consequence of workers' generalised insecurity and uncertainty due to high unemployment and the limited extent to which their rights are protected as a result of the deregulation of labour relations has been a decrease in workers' collective action. On the one hand, workers in full-time, steady jobs tend to identify their interests with those of the enterprise so as to safeguard their positions, and

it is difficult for workers in flexible forms of employment to join traditional trade union organisations or to create new ones to represent themselves only. On the other hand, all that people outside the employment system can hope for is certain degraded work activities offered to them from time to time. It is particularly difficult for this segment of the labour force to express itself collectively. Trade union participation is essentially limited to groups of full-time workers in steady jobs whom the unions organise and represent, mostly at company level. These characteristics of the trade union movement and the weakening of collective action have allowed the employers' side to obtain consent for its choices, and, despite increased social inequalities, the system of labour relations appears to be consensual.

Context: Training/Skills/Knowledge

General Skills	4	At the same time, enterprises' increased demand for specialised but multi-skilled workers exerts pressure in the direction of reform of the systems of education and training. In their practice, however businesses will continue to be cautious and to limit themselves to piecemeal business activities. A system for diagnosing educational needs and introducing training specifications is being adopted and implemented, and training providers are specialising by subject, industry and specific geographical range. Training providers are concentrating chiefly on improving educational methods and techniques, on carrying out training and on evaluating their trainees. They are forced to become more competitive and to specialise their training services, in order also to ensure their viability.

In-company training	4	The process of restructuring the Greek economy has an impact on production in specific sectors and enterprises. Thus it increases the need for planning in-company training on the sectoral and/or enterprise level, and meeting specific institutional and structural needs of enterprises in order to boost their competitiveness. The necessary restructuring of the organisational model of enterprises requires the inclusion of in-company training in enterprises' business plans and its readaptation to the needs of enterprises in new knowledge and skills. Medium-sized and large enterprises have realised that vocational training may act as a means of integrating workers in the enterprise's value system and help boost its productivity.
Willingness to invest	4	Many enterprises fail to implement integrated business strategies by supporting their work force. The appearance of social inequalities, a result of the fragmented restructuring of the economy and the reinforcement of active employment policies, causes an increase in private spending on training. The number of enterprises that finance training of their workers has increased, but this applies mainly to large enterprises. Community and national funding for training remains an important parameter of the system, but is not addressed to the work force as a whole.
Life long learning	4	The part played by commercial training providers is more effective, since their range and scope of training activity are specific and they have increased the margins and incentives of their investment. Vocational training has been integrated in a total strategy to boost employment and in development policy, by acquiring a more regulatory, stabilising role. Its benefits, apart from the educational grant, are focused on more substantial results in relation to employment, social inclusion and the alleviation of social inequalities.

A more effective combination of training and information services and consultative orientation to a specific jobs offers strengthens the role of training as a means of enhancing access and inclusion of social groups threatened by exclusion.

Information and communication technologies have been extensively introduced to learning. That is why emphasis is laid on qualifications and skills, regardless of the different learning paths and the means of achieving them, which however meet prescribed specifications.

The new technologies, which will facilitate learning and information, are bringing about a more rapid reform of education and training programmes, and a redefinition of the role of teachers. The constant increase in the number of IT users and increased market demand for the relevant specialities have an impact both on the content of studies and on learning techniques.

8.1.4.3. Scenario III – Competitive economy – life long learning – new dimensions in social policy

DESCRIPTORS	QUANTITATIVE DESCRIPTION	QUALITATIVE DESCRIPTION
Context: Economy		
Restructuring	5	The process of restructuring the economy has come to an end, and has had a strong, universal impact on the economy and social organisation as a whole. Although the market is the basic regulatory factor in the sphere of the economy, the social dimension is taken into consideration when determining state policy, but mainly with regard to dealing with the effects of free market functioning. Also sought for in this framework are cooperation and consent between employers' and trade union organisations. Integrated, targeted policies are being formed,

		for intervening in the functioning of the economy and dealing with the effects of globalisation, through social dialogue processes. Restructuring is seen as a constant, unavoidable process, in the framework of which wage costs are a factor of secondary importance for boosting competitiveness. The primary sector is being revitalised as it moves away from mass production. Agricultural production is being restructured to accommodate high-quality, specialised products, which, thanks to well-developed sales networks, are sold on the global market (e.g. ecological products for personal consumption, pharmaceuticals). A large number of farmers combine the provision of tourism services with the production and sales of plant and animal products with appellations of origin. Thanks to the widespread use of technological innovations, all factors of production participate in the restructuring process.
Growth	5	Implementation of sectoral policies in the banking, insurance, food/beverages, tourism and non-metal products industries constitutes the framework for specialised enterprise-level development strategies. The parallel operation of horizontal policies in critical areas of the production process (development of networks, research, organisational innovations, development of continuing training and lifelong learning), has produced multiplier effects on sectoral policies. Manufacturing has acquired a strong sectoral specialisation in the sectors of food/beverages and chemical products, with extensive export activity in the Balkan and Mediterranean countries, as well as the countries of northern Europe. The banking and insurance sectors are based on provision of specialised products to enterprises. Tourism is being qualitatively improved and extended over a greater part of the year,

		providing a wide range of specialised tourist packages (eco-tourism, hiking, cultural and sports tourism, mountain tourism), mainly to the middle and upper income brackets in Europe.
Competition	5	The improvement and constant renewal of workers' knowledge and skills has been and is based on the requirements of international competitiveness, which is supplied by a broad network of specialised, flexible educational services. Knowledge, in the sense of its adaptation to the needs of enterprises and of the market more generally, is emerging as a central factor in development. The need for unskilled labour has been restricted to certain branches of the services sector. There are inflows of highly skilled immigrants from third countries, to meet the requirements of the economy.
Privatisation	3	The privatisation process has been completed and the public sector of the economy is restricted to meeting social needs. To safeguard its effectiveness, it relies on turning part of its operations over to private subcontractors, setting the framework for specific regulations regarding quality assurance and the objectivity of the services provided.
Demand for lower/mediate skills		The demand for low and mediate skills from enterprises is minimized. High level skills of the labour force are the key factor for the quality of the products and services and as a result, the competitiveness of the economy.

**Context:
Employment and labour market**

Flexibility/ mobility	4	With regard to employment and unemployment, changes have been noted in the composition of employment; to a degree, the statistical magnitude of unemployment has been reduced. From the aspect of the composition of employment, the share of public employment and employment in manufacturing has been

reduced significantly, and the share of employment in the non-state related services sector has increased. At the same time, the share of paid employment in total employment has increased significantly, with a parallel increase in both full-time, steady jobs and part-time casual and temporary jobs.

The fall in unemployment is due on the one hand to new job creation in growing industries, but on the other to the fact that a broad spectrum of people at the margins of the employment system are now regarded as regular workers.

Because of the high degree of deregulation of labour relations, the labour market shows a high level of flexibility and mobility; nevertheless, it ensures certain fundamental insurance rights for workers without a 'regular' job, and is acquiring a more 'dual' character.

| Work training patterns | 5 | On the one hand we have the great majority of the labour force, which, despite its strong internal differentiations regarding form of employment, pay, etc., is part of the employment system and enjoys at least a decent standard of living.
The development model, which has been adopted - improving competitiveness not by reducing labour costs but by upgrading workers and promoting worker participation, has resulted in an overall improvement in the financial and professional position of such workers. The price they have to pay for this is labour intensification and a drastic reduction in their free time, to which they agree for fear of being dismissed and finding themselves outside the employment system. In this framework, another common situation involves frequent changes of employer or job, or types of job that redefine the relationship between the workplace and the place of residence, such as telework and piecework rather than time-based work.
This improvement in the situation of a large part |

of the labour force has not come about as a result of central regulatory interventions aimed at protecting workers' labour and social rights, but as a result of the upward economic course taken by enterprises and the incentives they offer workers for as long as they remain within the system of employment. The state restricts itself to ensuring that even the weakest groups are equipped and given the opportunity to enter the system of employment, either as workers or as 'employable' people, thus shifting to the individuals themselves the responsibility for the course they will take in the future.

| Inequalities | 3 | A large segment of the labour force which has been underemployed in low-level jobs remains unemployed for long periods or has become inactive and marginalized. |

The functioning of the state in its social dimension aims at moderating the side-effects of the intensified social inequalities, without seeking to eliminate their causes. This is why the demand for social justice is translated into a demand for social sensitivity, and solidarity is understood to be everyone's ability to be offered opportunities. The discussion on equality of opportunity has replaced the discussion on the reality of the inequality of the results. In this framework, where the state no longer makes provision for reducing inequalities through the redistribution of income and the creation of a system of universal social protection for all citizens, as it did during the period of the post-war welfare state, the selective social measures for the weakest groups of the population - 'safety nets', 'subsistence incomes', etc. - have replaced social rights and express the prevailing social sensitivity; however they irrevocably stigmatise these weak groups.

Organisation of labour	5	The trade union movement has developed into a working component of the society of two-thirds, by representing the majority of employed earners who are in relatively steady employment.. This allows the labour relations system to function more on the basis of consensus. This development has led to social strife, which is once again gradually bringing the question of values back into the limelight - beyond the logic of the market - along with the questions of social justice, equality and solidarity.
Context: Training/Skills/Knowledge		
General Skills	4	In this socio-economic environment, vocational education and training have acquired decisive significance, both as inseparable elements of development policies, and as tools to give unemployed people the opportunity to enter or re-enter the system of employment.
		Training programmes are designed and readapted on the basis of specifically defined procedures for needs diagnosis and evaluation, in accordance with evolving occupational qualifications. They are meeting trainees' needs in a more flexible way, after individualised evaluations of their knowledge and experience.
		The requirements of enterprises for multi-skilled workers, the flexibility required in provision of training, and the new technologies all shift the responsibility for education and training onto the individuals themselves. At the same time, the organisation of the vocational training system itself helps reinforce the idea that learning is the responsibility of the individual.
		Training programmes are an integral part of development and employment promotion policies. They are implemented with greater flexibility, effectiveness and efficiency through the use of new learning technologies. They provide not only standardised and specialised knowledge, but also communications and initiative-taking skills, empowering workers to respond to the competitive

		and flexible division of labour. The demand for specialised knowledge and general adaptation skills is constantly increasing, and the definition of skills and their adaptation to market trends are ensured through reliable methods of diagnosing needs, which are developed and implemented with social consensus by state bodies and representatives of employers and workers.
In-company training	5	In-company training is an integral part of an enterprise's development plan. The new technologies facilitate provision of training to workers in a non-time-consuming and cost-efficient way. The results of in-company training are linked to improved labour and enterprise productivity.
Willingness to invest	5	Enterprises invest more and more in developing their work force as a decisive factor in introducing innovations to production, products and services. Small and medium-sized enterprises, either individually or jointly, conclude more substantial, more effective cooperation agreements with training providers.
Life long learning	5	Workers' general and social skills, acquired via different learning paths, are evaluated and recognised through commonly accepted procedures, and acquire intrinsic value in improving the situation and pay of workers. Demand and supply of qualifications, skills and aptitudes are harmonised, and the role of enterprises, government authorities and training providers is clearly delimited. Training providers are specialised in training methods and techniques which meet predetermined, commonly accepted standards for the qualifications, skills and aptitudes required. The effectiveness and adequacy of training providers is directly linked with their trainees' progress and career advancement. Distribution of training providers according to regional and local needs and according to the subjects and sectoral skills determined by market

trends leads to provision of specialised training services to meet demand.

Greater emphasis is placed on support for active employment policies, and on the increase and more rational exploitation of the resources to be made available for vocational training. The broader participation of private training providers and enterprises will ensure a greater increase in private spending on education and training. This will help increase the benefits and real results for employment promotion.

Despite the fact that its social character is limited, vocational training has an important role to play in the area of social inclusion for specific categories threatened with social exclusion. Its cultural dimension will be even further strengthened as a result of worker mobility and the inflow of economic immigrants.

By increasing their investment in manpower, enterprises are transformed into Learning Organisations and become more flexible, productive and competitive. Investment in manpower education/training is a matter for everyone, government organisations, enterprises and workers.

The systems of recognising and certifying skills have contributed to the simultaneous recognition of alternative forms of education and training, and provide workers with more opportunities for improving their qualifications on the job and outside the formal education system. On the other hand, they lead to individualised approaches both to training processes and to labour relations.

Setting educational standards based on vocational standards leads to a greater standardisation of training modules and their respective structures. It also forges a link between education, initial and continuing training programmes and the needs of the labour market. However, the organisation and standardisation of the vocational training system may lead to new inflexibility, unable to follow the development of skills and the rapid renewal of knowledge.

8.1.5. Luxembourg/Belgium

8.1.5.1. Scenario I – Controlled Globalisation

DESCRIPTORS	QUANTITATIVE DESCRIPTION	QUALITATIVE DESCRIPTION
Context: Economy		
Restructuring	5	As in the eighties, globalisation is the main goal. Policy makers focus on developing global markets and global production systems. In this ultra-liberal and highly competitive context, the State retires from a some parts of its responsibilities. The cooperation between public and private organisations decreases ceaseless and the largest part of the decisions in the economic, industrial and commercial domains, are influenced by the private decision-makers, considered to be more effective. However, the growth does not know its expected development. The State still keeps a role of regulation, but reduced to the bare minimum.
Growth	4	Growth is especially supported thanks to the development of the competitiveness on behalf of SMEs, which take one more important place in the economy of the country, in spite of an ever growing dependence to the large companies. The market governs in spite of the regulation role kept by the State, but in the final, companies and microeconomics has most importance. SMEs, always very dependent on big companies for their activities, remain fragile on their funds and on their labour forces. Luxembourg develops its main production activities towards the developing countries which are more considered as producer and Luxembourg as consumer.

Competition	3-4	Moreover, the investment rate towards Luxembourg decreases whereas it increases towards the developing countries. From the European point of view, Luxembourg economy is subjected to a constant Community influence, and the political and economic integration of the Grand-Duchy in the European Union knows a constant increase.
Privatisation	5	Since the middle of the first decade, the State removed its participation of the last national companies to let the market regulate the economic activity.
Context: Social Labour		
Flexibility/ mobility	5	The needs for foreign labour forces still exists for people with high qualifications because of the increase of the average age level. Migrants from the bordering countries (France, Germany…) are no more the only labour forces needed but the Union plays a weak role in the mobility of competence. Work contracts are custom-made according to the qualification and the profile defined by the companies.
Work training patterns	4	Concerning employment, a wide range of new custom-made contracts allows access to work for numerous categories of workers. Therefore, there are on the whole fewer outcasts but more precarity.
Inequalities	5	Unemployment increases in Luxembourg for under-qualified people as well as in the other developed countries or in the member States. The disparities (especially as regards to salaries, working conditions) will remain in progress, especially concerning women, young without qualifications, immigrants and the ones who do not adapt to the new technologies

Organisation of labour	2	On the legislative level, the State becomes very influenced by the market and by the biggest companies whose influence is at its highest level. Labour Law should adapt itself to the new reality of international competition and to the daily life of companies. Deregulation plays to the full. Fewer responsibilities, less rules, less rigidity, the organisation of work gradually starts to be become more and more independent from State regulations. These are directed towards the responsibility of the companies which can elaborate working schedules without any control, as well as they can define their own recruitment policies.
Context: Training		
General skills	3	The State is no more responsible for lifelong training. It does not insure more than basic education, common to all the citizens. Companies are in charge of vocational training, and define themselves their own policies in terms of anticipated management of the labour forces and competencies.. The human resources have completely turned into a kind of capital of the company. In that case, women, young without qualifications, immigrants and the ones who do not adapt to the new technologies have to face many difficulties to find a place on the labour market as they do not have access to lifelong training. In this context, the European Union plays also a significant role in the access to vocational training for the excluded categories. Nevertheless, disparities remain. The needs for general skills are at its lowest rate. Indeed, the main requirements are for social skills, which can be provided by the State.

In-company training	4	On the one hand, the employees of the big companies are favoured by this system. The managers have their taylor-made training programmes with adapted qualifications and contents with regard to the demands of the market. In this context, insofar as the State has gradually got rid off of its role with regard to in-company training, in fact the companies only decide of the investments to be carried out within the framework of vocational training. The European Union, by the means of subsidies and incentive programs to invest, proposes nevertheless a series of financial helps and incentive measures aimed at the companies.
Willingness to invest	4	On the other hand, In spite of efforts on behalf of SMEs to develop and to favour actions of training, employees of SMEs, for whom training is provided in an insufficient way, are obliged to take vocational training to their own charge. As the State has retired from its responsibilities, the legal rate obligation for companies to invest in training has been deleted, which implies that the amount of investment is based on the specific needs of each company. Finally, only the outcasts of the labour market can only take advantage of the basic education provided by the State.
Lifelong Learning	5	In a context of globalisation, lifelong learning will have a significant role to insure the links between competences and the needs for workforces by the companies. In the same way, lifelong learning will be one of the essential factors for employability and adaptation of the workers with the labour market.

8.1.5.2. Scenario II – State Regulation

DESCRIPTORS	QUANTITATIVE DESCRIPTION	QUALITATIVE DESCRIPTION
Context: Economy		
Restructuring	5	The world changes and globalisation of the economy dominates. The world becomes a wide chain of production of added value in which the last national companies, seeing the high development of private companies, try to hold their place. With the ever growing importance of new technologies, companies are now organised in networks, able to develop an important level of flexibility. A new cooperation is created between the companies which organise exchanges of goods and services.
Growth	5	The modification of certain legislative and regulatory aspects in the bordering countries allows the Luxembourger companies to a more important regional partnership (Saar-Lorraine-Luxemburg) and economic exchanges stressed within these partners. Moreover, beyond the development of the exchanges and regional co-operation, one notes an increasing influence of community intervention on Luxembourger economy. So one attends the birth of a progressive harmonization of the economic policies of the Member States, which starts to induce, at the level of Luxembourg, a passive attitude, guided by the choices and the decisions of the supranational authority.
Competition	3-4	The new system of production generates many job opportunities and consumption knows a steady growth The social situation has changed and the State manages to do an effort of adaptation. Nowadays, it does not intervene to make the

		major decisions but to intervene as a guarantee factor of the vested interests. Considering the measures which it takes to follow the change, it becomes a guarantee factor in terms of salaries and of working time. Henceforth, it has a responsibility to support employment and work statutes. The major decisions from now on are made at the supranational level, and the State preserves a role of regulator in the implementation of these decisions.
Privatisation	5	More and more, the State will retire its participation within the last national companies so to as to let the market regulates. The national leaders decide on an opening on the world, in order to follow the accelerated globalisation of the companies.
Context: Social-Labour		
Flexibility/ mobility	5	The evolution of the working modes, led by the generalisation of the new technologies, leads to a new social situation. Flexibility and the evolution of work brought many diversified personal situations. The State, under the influence of the European Union, as a response to the new working forms and to the new economic relations, answers by adjusting the legislative framework.
Work training patterns	5	Unemployment rate is still very low (close to 3%) and the need in foreign workforces is still a topical question. Seeing the developments of the bordering countries (especially France) new social aspirations appear : working is not the main value any more. So as to give an answer to these new aspirations the State responds by reducing the daily duration of working which implies an ever growing need in workforces.

Inequalities	3	With the appearance of new exigencies concerning the professional life, the disparities among men and women are reduced but do not totally disappear, notably as regards to the access to the prestigious jobs or as regards to the ladders of salaries. In terms of unemployment, the persons with low level of qualification stay the most concerned ones.
Organisation of labour	5	Moreover, one notices the appearance of long training phases or non-working phases which, henceforth, which go along with the normal path of a career and an active life. Also, the demand of leisure time grows: partial work-time, reduced work-time, chosen work-time…, thus, personal aspirations tend to overcome the professional life which remains nevertheless the essential factor of the personal well-being. Negotiations take place within the companies concerning the reduction of working time, this not to reduce unemployment, which remains relatively low, but to bring improvements to the quality of life.
Context: Training		
General skills	2-3	There is no strong demand for general skills literally. Nevertheless these general skills are part of priorities for the State which sees there a way of reducing the inequalities. The demand for social skills is on the other hand very strong, because it is synonymic of integration for the workers. With the new organisation of labour, the general skills are often guarantors for an effective vocational training.
In-company training	5	As an answer to the social aspiration and to the change of work organisation, the State adapts itself. The national contributions are completed by contributions intended to fund the training periods or non-working phases. Also, with the

		division of the structures and the organisation of companies in networks, the weight of training and individual training programs increases. With regard to the previous part, individuals will see their progress of professional life modified and interrupted more and more by periods of part-time work, of more or less extended training periods.
Willingness to invest	4-5	The excluded of the labour market (young without qualifications, immigrants, 50-year-old people...) are given a great opportunity by the measures taken by the State and the companies, which encourage them to get professional qualifications by funding training. Moreover, the individuals are more and more incited to participate, financially speaking, in the vocational training. Training in this context is not seen as a factor of adaptation to the work place but as a way of perpetual social development linked with the new social aspirations.
Lifelong Learning	5	By the means of lifelong learning, the State allows the excluded from the labour market to get with a second chance of professional qualification. Beyond this aspect, lifelong learning is made necessary so as to insure the mobility and employability of the workforces.

8.1.5.3. Scenario III – Proximity of Training

DESCRIPTORS	QUANTITATIVE DESCRIPTION	QUALITATIVE DESCRIPTION
Context: Economy		
Restructuring	5	In those days, the development of the production of goods and their exchange consolidates the commercial regionalisms around the traditional most important productive regions (North America, Europe, Asia) but also new ones (South America).
Growth	4-5	Growth is at a high level and at every level (local, international…), efforts are made to give the individuals the benefits of it. Work and employment systems (and in continuous training) will get the greatest benefits of this change. A better repartition of the growth throughout the world is realised and even the developing countries meet this increase of growth.
Competition	3	But all these poles of production and business are based on a new economic order throughout the world. The European Union, now completed with new member states, organised around the single currency, widens and strengthens its relations with the rest of the world and all these Member States, including Luxembourg, benefit from this new organisation. All these partners have as an objective the research for global performance Also, the introduction of Euro at the beginning of the decade strengthened the economic weight of Europe and of its member states, which appear henceforth as the main economic competitors of the United States.

Privatisation	5	The standard of living is more stable and the average salary in Luxembourg is still the highest in Europe. The level of qualification of the employees required has reached a high level, that implies a perpetual training to meet the needs.. More and more, the State retires its participation within the last national companies so to as to follow the accelerated globalisation of economy.
Context: Social-Labour		
Flexibility/ mobility	5	With the new cooperation spirit, the individuals have to be flexible. The former model of the work place has disappeared and nowadays, the individuals have to spend a part of their working time in other companies. The organisation of the companies in networks also implies new needs. Nowadays, social skills are prevailing at the same level as technical skills.
Work training patterns	5	Technological progress is so fast that knowledge and competencies become quickly obsolete, which implies a willingness to train continuously and to develop the employability of individuals. The careers are not linear any more. The progress of a professional career will be inevitably interrupted by long training periods, by periods of retraining or experiences in other companies or even by non-working periods.
Inequalities	3	A new conception of employee appears in this spirit of co-operation. The work-forces are no more only a cost factor for the company, they become a factor of enrichment which needs training and re-training perpetually. At the local level, Luxembourg undertakes massive efforts in favour of the insertion of the excluded from the labour market, and particularly people with low qualifications. The State, the regional and local actors, in this perspective, play an incentive role for the access of the excluded of the labour market.

Organisation of labour	5	The situation of strong growth induced by the world co-operation has consequences at the micro-economic level. The companies try to convey this spirit of co-operation and anticipation to their staff. Everything changes, the organisation of work, working conditions, people's expectations. The complete organisation of work is rethought, recomposed. Part-time work, multifunctional work tasks or individualised working time frames require important.
Context: Training		
General skills	4-5	In this context, the State, the local institutions, and all the organisations (professional chambers, social partners) involved in the economic dimension play a key role. To ensure the management of the periods of training and the periods of work, 'collection of incomes' is necessary. Under the influence of the co-operation and the higher rating of the human resources, as well as under some local measures to facilitate access to the labour market for excluded people, several support mechanisms are therefore focusing on training and employability measures.
In-company training	5	Initial training is not the reference anymore. The companies tend to favour social skills of the individuals, even if the qualifications still keep their importance. Therefore, vocational training becomes the major preoccupation for managers to adapt people to the workplace. It is not considered as an expense anymore but as an investment. Nevertheless, the investments of companies in training are going especially to benefit in the salaries of enterprises. Indeed, as far as companies are going more to recruit co-workers in an optics of provision of a service, these are not going to benefit from investments realized by companies.

Willingness to invest	5	The measures to favour the investment of companies in the training measures become more important under the rhythm of growth. The companies, convinced of the importance of training, for their development, increase the allowance for training and at instigation of the State which increases its participation in the financing. Finally, according to the example of some of its neighbour countries, Luxembourg sets up a series of measures aiming at the collection of incomes to finance training. The participation of companies in the actions of training is henceforth dominant.
Lifelong Learning	5	So as to insure a durable social cohesion, lifelong learning plays a particularly significant role. Initially, it makes it possible to fight against under qualifications by developing the capacities of social and professional mobility. But beyond this aspect of professional mobility, it ensures a better employability and a better social protection of the individuals.

8.1.6. Poland

8.1.6.1. Scenario I – Limited Development/Ad hoc Adjustments

DESCRIPTORS	QUANTITATIVE DESCRIPTION (¹)	QUALITATIVE DESCRIPTION
Context: Economy		
Growth	3	World market business climate is not very favourable to Polish economic development. Average annual GDP growth rate of about 4,5 %, higher by 2 % than in the EU countries, will make Poland reach 45-50 % of the average GDP level per one EU inhabitant, taking into account the current Union Members. Regional development differences are not reduced but become more striking in many cases. Due to the delay in the EU accession until after 2005, Poland may not benefit from the participation in the EU structural policy. The pre-accession assistance makes no significant contribution to the reduction of regional differences in development levels.
Economic restructuring	3	The economy is restructured mostly under the influence of market forces. The government takes up active restructuring of the economy only in the selected, problem-posing sectors. The IT and communication services' sector is gaining in importance but its development is dominated by large international corporations. The restructuring and modernization of agriculture is initiated following preparations for the European Union membership but it does not produce significant results. Both the agriculture and the agricultural environment get modernized to a certain degree. The management in the area of agriculture gets improved and so does the

(¹) The below-mentioned descriptor values refer to the intensity evaluation of a given descriptor in a specific scenario.

		know-how. Although, the market structures are developed and the multi-function development of agricultural areas is stimulated, the agricultural structure does not change to a great extent.
Competition	4	The competition among enterprises becomes clearly diversified. Increasing globalisation, no possibilities of investment in production modernization, as well as high employment costs make the situation difficult for most of the enterprises and, in particular, the SMEs. The companies' competitiveness becomes increasingly dependent upon intangible values (rather than the material ones) including know-how, development potential and potential of the employees. IT and communication techniques. Development conditions are more favourable for the foreign capital-related companies transferring the know-how from better developed countries. The most competitive companies are the ones able to take advantage of 'knowledge management'. Some of the companies make skilful use of the existing possibilities of supporting their development within the development programmes financed by the government and the European Union. However, this is mainly the case of well-off companies being able to take advantage of the assistance offered to them.
Privatisation	3	The privatisation process is carried out on an ad hoc basis. It aimed mainly at attracting direct foreign investment in order to improve the payment balance. At the same time, the important social circles become more and more convinced that the privatisation does not bring about the expected results and that is advantageous mostly for the elites. The participation of private sector in GDP is gradually growing to reach 75 % in 2005 and 90 % in 2010.

Context: Social Context/Work		
Flexibility/mobility	2	There are still some internal economic barriers restraining the mobility of employees. The domestic mobility mainly refers to highly qualified employees. Their transition periods are established for the mobility of Polish employees within the EU after Poland's accession. In practice, the mobility of employees having lower/average qualifications is limited while the highly qualified employees, demanded for in the Western labour markets, may find employment opportunities in those markets. There is a noticeable 'brain drain' in those categories.
Work/Training	3	Relations between the labour market needs and the workforce supply are not based on long-term forecasts and plans. Large employing establishments and, in particular, the foreign capital-related ones take over the methods of the 'learning organisations'. Generally speaking, however, the training is not a priority and it lags behind the activities aimed at product development and marketing. The workplaces are usually more careful about the managers' training than about the professional development of other employees. Due to the educational system reform, there are many extensively qualified young people coming into the labour market but they usually have no practical skills. A majority of employers are not prepared for the employment of such people.
Inequalities	4	Although the employment growth is rather moderate, unemployment reaches a high stable level significantly exceeding the EU average. The number of young unemployed people is particularly high. The threatened and socially excluded groups are getting more and more numerous. The level of an undisclosed unemployment is still high (4-5%). The inequalities in work and education availability between towns and villages are getting grosser.

Work Organisation	3	In a majority of enterprises, the globalisation of economy does not result in work organisation changes. Traditional management patterns and hierarchical structures are dominant. More extensive modifications are introduced in enterprises known as 'economic leaders' and in foreign capital-related companies. Legal conditions are created in order to enable the enterprises to employ people for a definite time period, for the purpose of executing a specific task but such form of employment very slowly gains popularity.
Context: Training		
General Skills	3	'General skills' are less appreciated by the employers who are still searching for employees educated in a particular profession, specialization (just like in the preceding socio-economic system). It seems that, in such development scenario, general skills are more important for the employees who foresee that the improvement of economic situation, and faster economic growth will allow for their better use, retraining or finding a better job (and they also may be useful in given circumstances). A similar attitude is presented by some of graduates starting their first job and by certain students hoping to get a better job in the future (but also connecting the development of general skills with their personal development - irrespective of their job). Taking into account certain arrears in educational system (curricula, equipment) and former working which did not always encourage to develop such skills, the needs in this area are impressive. The refer mainly to: foreign language skills, computer literacy, Internet use, a number of social, communicational and interpersonal skills.

In-company Training	3	Vocational education needs of enterprises are limited mainly by the economic situation of the said companies but also of the whole State. A decreased demand for labour force, labour force surpluses in certain areas (high unemployment level) and the lack of system-related solutions in such field as: vocational education - employing establishment do not force the majority of enterprises to get interested in educational opportunities for their own needs. However, there are certain dynamically developing areas, some of which actively invest in personnel training. The fact that it is relatively rarely possible to acquire some practical professional skills through an enterprise is an obvious obstacle for students or workers wishing to learn, re-train or upgrade their skills. In certain professions it is simply impossible to acquire skills outside the workplace.
Willingness to invest	2	Individuals are definitely less inclined to invest in vocational education and training due to a weak motivation, effectiveness of training as a means of promotion and a manner of taking up a job. The educational activity of individuals is usually aimed at a personal development and it does not bring any benefits such as a better job, promotion or higher remuneration. A deeper involvement of national, local/regional authorities in education (organisation and financing) is required mostly by the trade unions. State institutions try to meet some part of those requirements. Little action is taken by enterprises and employers.
Lifelong Learning	4	In a lower-growth-rate scenario the needs of an individual, employer, VET organizer and the State relating to life long learning are reduced due to a lower rate of depreciation of the knowledge acquired by students and workers. The 'educational gap' which stems from the

discrepancies between professional preparation (mostly at a school of enterprise level with respect to the 'initial training) and the technology of a given profession are growing at a moderate rate. Thus, it does not result in a sudden withdrawal from the said profession.
Psychological reasons for life long learning of individuals have not yet been fully developed and they refer only to certain people, the majority does not appreciate nor realize the importance of life long learning.
Both the State and the employer stress mainly the current educational needs. The school forms of VET are focused mostly on initial training. The essential financing sources in the area of life-long learning (the State, employers, foundations and individuals) consist of the State entities and various foundations (including the international).

8.1.6.2. Scenario II – Growth, Cooperation and Competition

DESCRIPTORS	QUANTITATIVE DESCRIPTION (¹)	QUALITATIVE DESCRIPTION
Context: Economy		
Growth	4	World market business climate is favourable to Polish economic development. Average annual GDP growth rate of about 6% allows for approaching the European Union average. The EU accession gives an opportunity of a further increase in the said growth rate (1.5-2%). In 2010, Poland makes its GDP amount to at least 60% of the average EU level. Poland's EU accession before 2005 makes it possible to include the country soon in the EU structural policy and to obtain a considerable assistance in that area (€ 6-8 billion a year). It may exert an important influence upon Poland's

		balanced development.
Foreign investment volume is growing from the moment of Poland's EU accession and investors start to feel more secure.
Economic Restructuring	5	The State actively participates in restructuring the economy. The government, in particular, adopts a firm policy to modernize the economic structure. Such actions are aimed at the development of sectors generating high added values and services, especially, the IT and communication ones thus modernizing the GDP generating structure.
The participation of the service sector in employment structure exceeds 50% and the participation of SMEs reaches the level of 70-75%.
Agriculture restructuring and modernization will be initiated but the proportion of the number of people (officially) employed in agriculture to the total number of workers decreases only from the current 27% to slightly less than 20% in 2010. The agriculture becomes structurally polarized into the units economically weak and into the ones able to act individually. Nevertheless, it will be possible to reach the current EU standards in the field of agriculture within the next 20 years at the earliest.
Competition	3	In order to gain or maintain a competitive market position, the enterprises become increasingly dependent on the added value generated through the application of the scientific research results. In part with assistance of the European Union, the State actively implements a generally available policy in support of human resources development, especially in the least developed areas and in those affected by high unemployment level.
The disproportion existing between economic leaders on one hand and State enterprises, the budget sphere and companies operating in less

developed regions - on the other and referring to the investment in human resources is gradually removed.

The State implements, to the extent admitted by the EU legislation, a policy of supporting the development of the economic areas characterized by the highest growth rate of demand for their services and products, such as: company services, high-tech industries; manufacturing and services referring to leisure activities, as well as health and environmental protection products and services.

The export structure is changed for the benefit of high-tech products and services.

Privatisation	5	The privatisation process is being carried on and its rate increases. It also becomes an element of a unified economic policy providing for tax reduction, as well as for the limitation and reallocation of public expenses. The participation of private sector in GDP is growing to reach 90% in 2005.
Context: **Social Context/Work**		
Flexibility/ mobility	4	Domestic mobility of employees is still limited although more advantageous conditions are being created e.g. through the housing construction development. Barriers for the international mobility of Polish employees, provided for in the accession treaty, are quickly removed due to their irrelevance. Conditions are created for combining education and training periods and employment. There is a significant increase in the participation of workers showing flexibility in responding to the labour market changes. People will perform limited-time jobs at home - using the telecommunication techniques (tele-work), on temporary basis, upon summons etc.

Work/Training	4	Business circles become more and more responsible for vocational training and development. Cooperation networks are established at regional/local level between the business environment and vocational education and training organizers. The enterprises identify their training needs in a more effective way revealing the results to vocational education and development organizers and enabling them to adjust their offer to the labour market needs in a more appropriate way.
Inequalities	3	The number of workplaces is increasing considerably. Although the unemployment gets reduced, it still remains rather high (7-8%) mostly in proportion to the growing number of people in a productive age. The unemployment among old people becomes grosser, as employers prefer young workers. The inter-occupational mobility of older people is also smaller. Poorly qualified people find it more difficult to get a job. Although the threat of social exclusion does not increase, the number of the unemployed becomes stable. However, there is little possibility of improvement.
Work Organisation	4	The globalisation, increasing competition and the wide use of IT and communication techniques make most enterprises apply flexible and efficiency-raising solutions. Outsourcing and lean production are getting more and more common. The extent to which a tele-work is used is increasing, although on a much smaller scale than in the case of highly developed countries. The employment for a definite period of time and for the performance of a particular task will get much more common and so will the part time jobs.

Context: Training		
General Skills	5	Employers are more appreciative about general skills of workers applying for jobs. The areas of economy which are based mostly on knowledge (both a specialized and a general one) are gaining in importance. An increased mobility of workers, introduction of modern technologies, and an extensive globalisation on various levels (information, production, sales etc.) result in a relative decrease in the importance of professional skills and, in particular, the simplest ones. On the other hand, general skills are getting more and more important and, in many cases, they are a necessary condition for vocational education for the purpose of high-technologies. More importance is attributed to social skills (competence) such as: team-working, social adaptation to changing conditions (change of profession) or development (starting from the school level) of the skill to enter the labour market (job-search, entrepreneurial activity, preparing CV, etc.). The VET organizers are also more concerned about the development of different forms of vocational guidance.
In-company Training	4	Owing to the improved economic situation (considerable GDP growth dynamics, unemployment reduction and significant limitation of the inflation), there is an increase in a skilled labour force. Enterprises are not always able to avail themselves of a staff which would satisfy their needs concerning both the number and the area of professional qualifications. In many cases, enterprises start striving for workers and they develop vocational education. It seems however that, the growing interest of employing establishments in vocational education and training stems mainly from a

system solution in the area of in-company training of employees. The state budget can afford to refund to enterprises the costs of education, training and re-training of students or workers. It is a certain financial burden for the State but also an advantage for students (employees) and employers. Students, candidate employees, are willing to learn 'true' technologies in 'true' circumstances (which is very much the same in the field of tangible and intangible services). This is often the first time they can get in touch with high-technology at the level which could not be available at any school. Employees are financially motivated to care for an appropriate education level and it refers both to the education quality and terms (financial, organisational, cultural etc.).

Willingness to invest	4	Individuals are interested in bearing their education costs, there is a significant development of the educational services' market (mostly the non-public one). Due to the economic situation and certain system-related solutions (see: „in-company training) employers are getting more and more involved in vocational education. The role of authorities at both central and lower levels is becoming less important. An increasing demand for vocational education and in-company training may also affect the amounts of payments made by individuals in the specialities and professions being subject to the VET organizers' competition. The unitary training costs may drop. In the case where a monopoly is held by a small number of training centres (rare professions, specialities) and the demand is increasing - prices of certain educational services may increase.
Lifelong Learning	5	A fast growth may result in tensions in certain fields of economy, professions and specialities (the 'educational gap' may even become an 'educational gulf'). All the four key life-long

learning actors (individual, employer, VET organizer and the State) are insisting on the development of that form of skills' upgrading. Individuals are getting more and more conscious about the role of life-long learning which results in establishing a certain tradition. It is an important discriminant of cultural changes as regards refreshing one's knowledge, changing speciality and professional re-training.

In the case of an increased growth rate, the State, employers and workers are ready to bear the specific professional upgrading costs. They are usually conscious of the fact that such costs are relatively small as compared to the increase in an employee's work efficiency and the costs of training of a 'new' specialist (from the very beginning).

The demand for various life-long learning forms may result in an entry into the domestic market of foreign companies dealing with organisation and implementation of professional skills' refreshing and upgrading process.

8.1.7. Slovenia

8.1.7.1. Scenario I – Economic and Social Crisis

DESCRIPTORS	QUANTITATIVE DESCRIPTION	QUALITATIVE DESCRIPTION
Context: Economy		
		The membership of the new CE and EE countries overburdens the EU funds, and with the recession and some elements of new protectionism in the EU, the reforms in the new member countries are slowed down.
Restructuring	2	The transformation of the majority of Slovenian companies is stopped. Those companies who went through the restructuring process faster

		have better starting point than slower companies. The differences between Slovenian companies are growing. Because of the recession successful Slovenian firms as well as those who are not successful are easy targets for the foreign take-overs.
Growth	2	After a relatively long period of steady economic growth and after becoming the member of the European Union, a new cycle of economic crisis also strikes the Slovenian economy. Slovenian government loses control over the harmless harmonisation of the industrial sectors with the EU economy and some of the sectors are strongly affected by that.
Competition	2	Economic crisis slows the process of adaptation of Slovenian firms to global competition. Globally, Slovenian companies are less competitive than 10 years ago. The infrastructure of social partnership built in the past period is partially destroyed and new antagonisms between social partners (especially between trade unions and employers) rise again.
Privatisation	3	Privatisation of the former public enterprises is finished, but in order to regain some control over the economic situation, the state considers getting back some influence in publicly important areas.
Context: Labour market		
Flexibility/ mobility	3-4	Successful firms that are already on the global market, and are using the new IC technologies, are flexibly organised and have flexible and well-skilled workforce. Geographical mobility of the workforce inside the country increases, but there are several barriers to labour mobility on the EU level. Most of the firms (SMEs) that are oriented to the domestic market lack the means for the modernisation and are taking the steps of numeric flexibilisation to reduce the workforce.

Organisation of work	3	For the majority of companies new crisis means reducing the size of the workforce, new cuts in employment and strengthening of the hierarchical structure. The state adopts new measures to further deregulate the conditions on the labour market.
Work/training patterns	5	Employers seek mainly for the young workers who are able and willing to work under conditions and rules set by the employers. Temporary work is predominant pattern for newly employed workers. Since the restructuring of the Slovenian economy is not finished and the share of the industry in the economy is still relatively high, there is still need for low skilled workers. Nevertheless, highly skilled and flexible workers are still needed. There is an open competition between companies for experts specialised in particular areas.
Inequalities	3	This, as a consequence, deepens the segmentation of the labour force. Economic crisis accelerates social differentiation and increases the occurrence of social inequality. The number of the unemployed rises again. At the same time there is a reduced number of vacancies and relatively closed new employment, which brings down some positive effects of demographic changes (ageing of the labour force and decreasing population) that would normally increase the demand for the available (even older) labour force.
Context: Training		
		Educational institutions are also in crisis. The ongoing process of educational reform, which should contribute to the closer link between the labour market demands and the educational system, is slowed down by the lack of finances.

General Skills	2-3	To provide general and transferable skills to as many people as possible, the state increases the centralisation of the educational system (the provision and organisation of education).
In-company training	2	Many providers of education can not afford to include the IC technologies in the educational process. This raises the importance of the in-company training, which could be afforded only by more successful (larger and medium sized) companies and for the specific needs (only for their core workers).
Willingness to invest	2	The employers are trying to withdraw from providing the training places and apprenticeship places for students of vocational and professional programmes, and are asking the state for finances to support training in the working environment. Individuals are rarely prepared to invest in education and training. For those activities are interested only already highly educated and skilled individuals.
		On the policy level, the methodological approaches for anticipating the training needs and the demands of the labour market, and the methodological tools for evaluating the existing educational programmes, are still largely missing. The demographic changes increase the importance of certification system and educational programmes for adults. On the other hand, the increased demand for younger workforce causes a high drop-out from regular education or lover rate of continuing education.

8.1.7.2. Scenario II – Slow and Steady (controlled) Growth

DESCRIPTORS	QUANTITATIVE DESCRIPTION	QUALITATIVE DESCRIPTION
Context: Economy		
		EU membership does not influence much the situation in the Slovenian economy.
Restructuring	4	The situation on Balkan improves and many Slovenian companies find new, promising and not so demanding markets for their products and services. Consequently that slows down the process of restructuring and adapting to the global competition. Smaller companies seek complementary partners for outsourcing and merging in order to improve the production and to increase their share on the market. Some industrial sectors are more affected by the EU membership, but the government provides the measures that help to alleviate the losses.
Growth	4	The annual growth of GDP is about 3% and is controlled by the state measures.
Competition	3-4	Successful companies are stimulated, but in some cases the government still byes social peace by helping 'the weakest' out. Financial support from the structural funds is not used selectively and efficiently and public administration is still big, expensive and not very efficient. Actions from different state institutions (ministries and other bodies) are not fully harmonised yet. Consequently, some successful Slovenian companies are globally competitive, but overall there is no big improvement in competitiveness comparing with the year 2000.
Privatisation	3	Communication between the social partners is regulated by the laws, but in practice the 'arguments of power' are stronger than the 'power of arguments'. The process of

		privatisation of large public companies is almost finished, but there is strong opposition to further privatisation. There is a fear that further privatisation of services would affect their quality.
Context: Labour Market		
Flexibility/ mobility	3	The Slovenian labour market is small, still mainly self-sufficient and relatively rigid. The laws introduced by the government to enable greater flexibilisation, at the same time, to some extent, protect the workers. Geographical and occupational mobility of the labour force is rising mainly on the regional and the state level.
Work/training patterns	4	The companies broadly use the IC technology. Employers emphasise the greater and more effective utilisation of the human resources, especially of the older workforce, by enhancing their education and skills. There is also greater demand for the general and transferable skills. Temporary employment (mainly for younger workforce) is still predominant pattern of flexible employment.
Organisation of work	3-4	With the growing number of companies and growing number of people employed in the service sector, the organisational structure of the companies is also changing (reducing the number of hierarchy levels, adapting to more flexible environment). R&D departments are gaining importance in more successful companies.
Inequalities	4	The growing demand of workforce reduces the number of the unemployed. Income inequalities and social differences are slowly increasing, but are understood mainly as the 'motivation factor' which keeps the unemployed in active search for employment.

Context: Training		
General skills	3-4	The educational system is still fairly centralised and that goes for the VET system too. The VET system is state controlled and regulated, but responsive to the skill needs of the companies and regions. Some of the educational programmes are modularised. Educational providers use the IC technologies in the education process and for the administrative purposes.
In-company training	3-4	The need for enhancing the education level and skills of the older workforce is usually detected and demanded by the employers, but in practice it is still expected that the education (for both, the youngsters and adults) will be mainly provided by the state. The in-company training is provided mostly for the core workers. Knowledge and skills acquired are recognised mostly on the internal markets (inside company). Internal training markets prevail.
Willingness to invest	3-4	Many of the providers are connected in the networks, which enable greater transparency and easier access to the programmes offered. Companies and regional structures as well as the educational providers occasionally analyse the labour market situation and the changing structure of labour demand, but there is still a lack of adequately qualified analysts.

8.1.7.3. Scenario III – Economic Growth and Flexibility

DESCRIPTORS	QUANTITATIVE DESCRIPTION	QUALITATIVE DESCRIPTION
Context: Economy		
		Slovenian membership in the EU brings new flow of capital to the Slovenian economy.
Restructuring	4-5	Slovenian government decides to adopt a flexible approach and to open the economy to the foreign investments. Companies are stimulated to seek partners abroad, to enter in the joint ventures or to integrate with the companies based on the common or similar production goals, and change the organisational structure to a more flexible one. The state stimulates creating SMEs. Introduction and proactive use of the IC technologies are also stimulated.
Growth	5	The annual growth of GDP is higher than 4% and the state does not undertake any special measures to control it. Finances from the structural funds are used selectively, efficiently and their usage is transparent. Greater discipline of the state and public administration is demanded and applied.
Competition	4-5	Overall economic and social situation increases the business opportunities for new entrepreneurs, especially those with new SME. Increased number of those companies increases the competition not only on the national but on the regional level too. Turnover rate of the companies is rapidly increasing.
Privatisation	4-5	Numerous privatised companies participate in the new social protection network with their services. Increased competition between them increases the quality of the services, but the access to the most groups at risk is still questionable.

Context: Labour Market		
Flexibility/ mobility	4-5	Companies are stimulated to be more flexible and to use all available means to be more effective and productive. The trade unions co-operate as long as these measures do provide new jobs and do not affect the basic rights of the workforce. Greater turnover rates of jobs and companies imply greater occupational and geographical mobility on the regional and national level.
Work/training patterns	4-5	For more effective utilisation of the labour force, more flexible and more educated and skilled workforce is needed. Greater demand (vacancies) for labour and smaller supply (ageing of the population) of the labour leads to the shortage of the available labour force. Measures for importing the needed labour force from abroad are implemented. New jobs are predominantly flexible, there is a growing share of the part-time employment. On the other hand, higher growth and prosperity create new set of permanent full-time jobs.
Inequalities	2-3	Greater turnover rate of jobs and companies threatens to accelerate the social differentiation and social inequalities. To deal with such consequences the new safety net (social protection) rules are introduced, and the social institutions are strict in implementing these rules. Social partners realise their role in ensuring the public welfare (besides defending their own interests) and they co-operate in achieving it. Specific unemployment rates, such as youth unemployment rate and older people unemployment rate, drop significantly. Due to labour force shortage more and more older people work, especially in the flexible patterns of employment (combinations of employment and retirement).

Organisation of work	4	The majority of the companies adopted different patterns of organisation, which are suitable to their needs and the characteristics of the workforce (team work, job sharing, strategic management, quality control, just-in-time production,...).
Context: Training		
General skills	4-5	Educational system adapts to be more flexible and responsive to the rapidly changing labour market needs. It is rather decentralised system, there are numerous providers of the educational and training programmes (for young as well as for adult population). Increased competition between those providers increases also the quality of the programmes. The IC technologies are used to achieve such goal. Labour market analyses are conducted on the regular basis and all labour market and education actors have qualified analysts. Databases on the national level are created and promptly updated. New transferable skills and competencies are integrated into curricula.
In-company training	4-5	Employers realise the importance of the life-long learning, in-company training, specialisation and regionalisation of education. They co-operate with the education providers in establishing the core skills and competencies needed for successful performance of jobs and in decentralisation of the educational system. The concept of the learning organisation is fully implemented.
Willingness to invest	4	The growing share of the older labour increases the importance of the certification system and non-formal types of education. Increased welfare enables different actors (especially individuals) to invest more in education and training. Older population is especially stimulated to participate in various education and training courses.

8.1.8. United Kingdom

8.1.8.1. Scenario I – Crisis Looms and the Big Players step in

DESCRIPTORS	QUANTITATIVE DESCRIPTION	QUALITATIVE DESCRIPTION
Context: Economy		
Restructuring	4	A consortium of industrial leaders has recently supported the election of a tough new centre-right government, brought in on a ticket of helping to restore economic prosperity through strong, positive intervention. The major multi-nationals are starting to take an economic and commercial lead, while state intervention is aimed at reforming regulatory frameworks, cutting down red tape, and educating and training a new elite that can lead others to grab the global opportunities.
Growth	4	After the steady economic success of the late 90s and early 00s, the economy faltered then took a dive. Domestic instability (made more turbulent through a wider global cycle, linked to oil production and instability in some world regions) resulted in a recession.
Competition	5	The UK economy had lost its competitive edge, productivity had declined in relative terms. Inward investment was evaporating fast, and even the profitability of the city was showing danger signs. The economic stakes, and risks, are high.
Privatisation	4	There is no further privatisation, and the public sector may regain importance.

Context:
Labour market and social dimension

Flexibility/ mobility	4	Neither employers nor the public sector were proactive in seeking change, so - except in a-typical situations - employees remained wedded to their traditional working practices - whether a fixed job or casualised. There was a reluctance to adapt, and the new government intends to step in here with a more dirigiste strategy
Work/training patterns	3	
Inequality/ exclusion	5	A lack of progress in the economy and in employment means that the 'haves' and 'have nots' are polarising, and the middle ground (in terms of skills and income) is falling away. One sign for optimism is that the earlier education reforms have addressed much of the basic skills deficit, at least among younger age groups.
Organisation of work	3	The Government is attempting to set a challenging steer for change in work organisation - a combination of inward, multi-national led investment and an environment for 'wiring up' SMEs to the securer, larger companies.

Context:
Demand for training

General skills levels	4	Once again skills shortages are seen as an important cause of the present economic difficulties. Businesses have relied on a low skills equilibrium, and until now not many firms have sought to introduce strategic change. Government has not given a lead over the 00s. While a minority of individuals and some regions and groups have made changes, this is not sustained across the society. If anything, skills are becoming more polarized.

In-company provision	3	A few companies continue to provide high quality training and professional development, though many smaller ones do not and never have. A particular problem here is that with growing instability and crisis, many multi-nationals have packed up their UK operations. The gap is widening.
Investment in training	3	Patchy at best - from individuals, firms and the public sector. Further more the human and capital investment needed to harness the opportunities of information technology to the full were missed, in the middle of the decade. 'New structures, up-skilling and new starts' is the new priority to get out of the downward spiral.
Lifelong learning	3	Much said, but little achieved until now. There has been growth in non-job related education - unemployment and an increasing sense of social cohesion in communities drive this. Increasing emphasis is placed on national and 'corporate' citizenship. The drive is to build on the improvements in basic education and equip employers with people who have IT and transferable skills. Individuals contribute substantially to the cost of HE qualifications.

8.1.8.2. Scenario II – Ad hoc Response to Global Pressure

DESCRIPTORS	QUANTITATIVE DESCRIPTION	QUALITATIVE DESCRIPTION
Context: Economy		
Restructuring	3	Open to the rigours of global competition, the UK government and industry reacted uncertainly, adopting short-term, specific responses.
Growth	2	Growth, at best, was modest The City has continued to prosper: assets held abroad helped to counterbalance weaknesses in the domestic economy. Some sectors also prospered cyclically, but manufacturing and agriculture remained in accelerating decline.
Competition	2	Competitiveness has declined further in the tough, global economy, although this pragmatic approach has not led to a sudden or drastic decline in economic performance or living standards.
Privatisation	3	Without a clear steer, successive governments adopted a cautious and short-term approach aimed to achieve consensus. The four home nations have adopted divergent stances.
Context: Labour market and social dimension		
Flexibility/ mobility	3	The trend towards flexible employment, self and part-time employment has continued, and this means that enterprises in some sectors adapted readily to immediate opportunities in the market. Investment in science, technology and human capital was insufficient to ensure that this development was sustained or applied to most sectors.

Work/training patterns	2	The relationship between skills needs and supply remained ad hoc - neither market signals nor planning were robust, so serious skills shortages and gaps remained. The relationship between skills needs and supply remained ad hoc - neither market signals nor planning were robust, so serious skills shortages and gaps remained.
Inequality/ exclusion	3	Inequalities remain a strong feature. While some groups still feel secure in their traditional niches, others were liable to sudden destabilisation and loss of employment. Successful workers have had to be mobile, versatile and, often, to multi-task. Social inclusion is claimed to be a priority but is not well-funded or well-organised except in areas which are deemed priority areas for new business starts.
Organisation of work	2	Industry and government became uncertain how to respond to global change Some development occurred, but traditional patterns prevailed as many firms and groups are slow to act or react. |//
Context: Demand for training		
General skills levels	3	Formal qualifications levels failed to keep abreast of the advances made by competitors in East and West Europe. There are other dimensions of difference in training provision. For example there is a clear national, regional and local dimension, which the government has encouraged and has claimed as successful.
In-company provision	2	The range of provision available in companies and colleges and through the web meant that a high proportion of employees could receive further training, mainly on short skills-based courses. In a few regions, notably where research and development in IT is strongest, there has been innovation and sustained development across the range of sectors. However, there is a lack of consistency across sectors and regions, and a lack of sustained goals and drive.

Investment in training	2	With no real national agenda, government departments and regional agencies played safe and rarely provided risk-based strategic planning. A mindset developed in schools, colleges and other public providers that they had to cover the main national training needs whilst others, free to experiment, could develop training in new areas of need.
Lifelong learning	2	Large employers see the situation as 'almost incoherent and lacking a pilot and navigator and sometimes a mission'. Notwithstanding this the divergent approach has led to some success stories. Some regions, driven by a social inclusion agenda, have made progress in engaging hard to reach groups in work-based training. Wales and Scotland have concentrated on their own agendas for education and training, and are benefiting strongly from this. Neither the role of the individual, nor 'citizenship' are articulated clearly.

8.1.8.3. Scenario III – A The free-market approach to competitiveness on course (UK Scenario 1)

DESCRIPTORS	QUANTITATIVE DESCRIPTION	QUALITATIVE DESCRIPTION
Context: Economy		
Restructuring	5	Competitiveness is driven by deregulation and the liberalization of market mechanisms. Flatter hierarchies aim to achieve profitability and a quick response to market change. The interest of entrepreneurs, shareholders and consumers dominates. A change of government confirmed UK's position on the periphery of the European project.

Growth	1	Growth was sustained in the market-driven economy. The City, finance and service sectors prosper strongly - media, some high technology industries, banking, insurance and other financial sectors, as well as personal and security services.
Competition	1	Government intervenes little, facilitating a culture that leaves the entrepreneur 'free'. These have been difficult times for some companies - including manufacturers and many SMEs.
Privatisation	1	Privatisation has continued, along with tax cuts and reductions in public spending.

Context:
Labour market and social dimension

Flexibility/ mobility	2	Emphasis has developed on the self-sustaining employee: employers reward value-added contributions more than loyalty. Flexibility implies here the mobile, part-time or portfolio worker. Only a minority of companies place emphasis on the high skills, versatile employee who develops as the company implements longer-term strategies. The labour force is mobile, while many traditional skills are redundant.
Work/training patterns	2	While some large companies operate as learning organisations, in many companies training lags behind product-market considerations and workforce management structures in terms of potential for gaining a competitive edge.
Inequality/ exclusion	3	Social tensions create a need for social inclusion measures. Working life is exciting, rewarding and risky for the majority who succeed and harsh for those who don't. Citizenship is seen as conformity to individualist norms and values.
Organisation of work	2	Companies adapt quickly and flexibly as reorganisations meet opportunities to expand and the need to contract. Flatter hierarchies aimed to achieve profitability, mainly concentrating on short-term opportunities.

Context: Demand for training		
General skills levels	3	Market signals - the skills employers will pay for and what qualifications people seek - generate an approximate skills balance, although some shortages and gaps remain. UK skills levels have improved, though the skills equilibrium is still at a lower level than in some other advanced economies.
In-company provision	2	Training provision is difficult to pin down as a structure. It is best appreciated as a dynamic network of users and providers; most of the latter are new companies, many based on former training and development units from large companies. Recruitment agencies are dominant in brokering training provision for companies of all sizes. Much of this tailoring of programmes and contracting providers is web-based.
Investment in training	2	Companies will invest in training where this has an immediate payback, but expect the state to take care of basic education and training for social inclusion. Individuals willing to pay have access to an extraordinary range of opportunities to learn through the web. Training vouchers can be borrowed from a Learning Bank, and individuals are expected to invest in their own training, as the rate of return can be high.
Lifelong learning	2	The emphasis is on the individual finding and making use of opportunities, rather than access for all; benefits to the individual are accentuated. Learning programmes are increasingly tailored to the needs of small groups of employees, while qualification-based courses are generally reserved for the early stages of people's learning careers. Learning programmes focus short interactive sessions on management processes and soft skills. Web-based opportunities proliferate in an individualist culture.

8.1.8.4. Scenario III – B A Social Partnership Approach to Competitiveness Develops (UK Scenario 3)

DESCRIPTORS	QUANTITATIVE DESCRIPTION	QUALITATIVE DESCRIPTION
Context: Economy		
Restructuring		The UK's earlier free-market approach softened by mid-decade, as government policy developed a stronger European dimension. Scotland has also forged wider European links. Stakeholder partnership is now accepted as the way to achieve the UK's economic and social goals. The interests of shareholders are generally balanced against the interest of stakeholders.
Growth		Economic development has been a success story. Multi-nationals are secure in the UK, and have many stable and profitable links with SMEs. The Euro settled after a bumpy start, and the EU is now enlarging with confidence.
Competition		Partnerships spot economic and social signals, both global and local.
Privatisation		Pressures to privatise are no longer strong. In any case, many services were already privatised, and there a loss of political and public confidence in wholesale privatisation.
Context: Labour market and social dimension		
Flexibility/ mobility		Outsourcing, downsizing and flexibilisation have continued. Their impact (on some social groups) has been mediated. Short/long-term developments are anticipated in negotiation between social partners, and this has enabled more firms to move towards long term strategies for building up the skills needed for a knowledge economy.

Work/training patterns		Skills gaps still exist, though less than one might have expected. Identifying and meeting skills needs is an important part of the government-led partnership process - though the UK's 'voluntarist' tradition and global pressures limit the amount of regulation of employment and earnings. Many people want to combine flexible working with their own chosen learning and lifestyles.
Inequality/ exclusion		Partnership promotes equity and opportunity; and tackling exclusion has become a priority. Emphasis is on stability, and protection from 'shocks'.
Organisation of work		The locally adapted variant of stakeholder partnership has, where successful, helped to establish learning organisations and new networks between co-operating firms. The inherent danger was that vested interests and cosy arrangements could dominate - partnership was not an easy option.
Context: Demand for training		
General skills levels		Training has responded to the market and in a buoyant economy the level of skills shortages are below what one might expect. However, the tendency remains for training remains 'third order' in terms of potential to bring about growth and effective competition.
In-company provision		In-firm training and private provision is important, alongside state-led programmes geared to help individuals meet changing skills needs. Private or public ICT access is widely used to enhance on-the-job learning.
Investment in training		Nationally funded provision and qualification development is regulated by government agencies through negotiation with social partners. 'Observatories' that combine research, analysis and policy formation are used to match

	skills to needs, but with varying success. Within this framework of provision decision-making at local level (regions and sectors) has thrived.
Lifelong learning	There is a strong emphasis on lifelong learning - though what exactly this is and how to achieve it remains elusive. National and regional citizenship is viewed as part of education and training. Individuals are expected to take significant financial responsibility for their own learning and training.

9. Annex II

9.1. Scenario/strategy methods

Scenario/strategy methods:
- as seen before the starting the project,
- as actually used in your project and
- as suggested on the base of the experiences of the project teams

Table A: **Steps**

STEPS AS SUGGESTED AT THE START OF THE PROJECT	STEPS AS ACTUALLY TAKEN IN YOUR PROJECT	STEPS AS YOU SEE THEM IN THE IDEAL SITUATION BASED ON YOUR EXPERIENCES
1. Defining the scope and the key questions.	Actual step: Information collected by: Short clarification:	Best step: Information collected by: Short clarification:
2. Identifying the major stakeholders.	Actual step: Information collected by: Short clarification:	Best step: Information collected by: Short clarification:
3. Identifying basic trends.	Actual step: Information collected by: Short clarification:	Best step: Information collected by: Short clarification:
4. Identifying basic strategy elements.	Actual step: Information collected by: Short clarification:	Best step: Information collected by: Short clarification:
5. Identifying key uncertainties, driving forces.	Actual step: Information collected by: Short clarification:	Best step: Information collected by: Short clarification:

6. Classification of the main developments according to importance and uncertainty. Aim is to find the two major developments that are the most important as well as most uncertain.	Actual step: Information collected by: Short clarification:	Best step: Information collected by: Short clarification:
7. Constructing initial scenario themes and matrices.	Actual step: Information collected by: Short clarification:	Best step: Information collected by: Short clarification:
8. Developing scenarios. General themes emerge from the simple scenarios and from checking them. Although the trends appear in all the scenarios, they can be given more or less weight or attention in different scenarios. At this stage not all scenarios need to be fleshed out.	Actual step: Information collected by: Short clarification:	Best step: Information collected by: Short clarification:
9. Checking for consistency and plausibility.	Actual step: Information collected by: Short clarification:	Best step: Information collected by: Short clarification:
10. Are there trends compatible within the chosen time frame?	Actual step: Information collected by: Short clarification:	Best step: Information collected by: Short clarification:
11. Do the scenarios combine outcomes of uncertainties that indeed go together?	Actual step: Information collected by: Short clarification:	Best step: Information collected by: Short clarification:

12. Are the major stakeholders placed in positions they do not like and can change?	Actual step: Information collected by: Short clarification:	Best step: Information collected by: Short clarification:
13. Evolving toward scenarios and robust strategies.	Actual step: Information collected by: Short clarification:	Best step: Information collected by: Short clarification:
14. Next we retrace the previous steps and see if the scenarios and strategies address the real issues facing the national VET-system.	Actual step: Information collected by: Short clarification:	Best step: Information collected by: Short clarification:
15. Are the scenarios relevant. to have impact, the scenarios should connect directly with the mental maps and concerns of the users.	Actual step: Short clarification:	Best step: Short clarification:
16. Are the scenarios internally consistent and perceived as such?	Actual step: Short clarification:	Best step: Short clarification:
17. Are the scenarios archetypal? They should describe generally different futures rather than variations on one theme.	Actual step: Short clarification:	Best step: Short clarification:

18. Are the scenarios describing an equilibrium, or a state in which the system might exist for some length of time?	Actual step: Short clarification:	Best step: Short clarification:
19. Test robustness of strategies in different scenarios.	Actual step: Information collected by: Short clarification:	Best step: Information collected by: Short clarification:
20. Strategic conversation: To develop these scenarios and strategies a strategic conversation should have taken place. 'It is the general conversational process by which people influence each other, the decision taking and the longer term pattern in institutional action and behaviour'. The national seminars were partly set up for this purpose.	Actual step: Short clarification:	Best step: Short clarification:

| 21. Institutionalisation: 'Ultimately the most effective way to ensure institutional effectiveness of the scenario process is for management to make the scenarios part of the ongoing formal decision making process'. The scenarios have to become part of the system for discussing strategic questions. | Actual step:
Short clarification: | Best step:
Short clarification: |

General comments on your experiences with the method:
-
-
-
-
-
-

10. Annex III

The questionnaire designed for EU-level stakeholders, can be found on the Max Goote website (http://www2.fmg.uva.nl/MGK/).

11. Annex IV

Outcomes overarching scenarios Cedefop

Cedefop suggests another set of scenarios, using two dimensions: socio-economic development and systemic divergence or convergence. Within each dimensions 2 possibilities are distinguished. Thus there are 4 scenarios in this 2x2 model. The overarching scenarios can be found in the table below.

Matrix: **Overarching scenarios on VET system's convergence or divergence in Europe**

SYSTEMIC DIVERGENCE OR CONVERGENCE \ SOCIO-ECONOMIC DEVELOPMENT	COMPETITION RATHER THAN COOPERATION	SOCIO-ECONOMIC COHESION
Liberalisation, decentralisation and individualisation	1. Competitiveness and splendid isolation: 'Divided Europe' Systemic divergences within and between countries remain and may increase; education/training systems and providers are in strong competition; increasing polarisation and marginalisation of certain target groups, regions, and sectors.	2. Unity in diversity: 'Pick and Mix Europe' The social and innovative role of education and training is recognised. However, no wider system development is taking place; systems and provisions develop only slowly towards mutual compatibility or transparency
Increasing convergence and mutual learning	3. Convergence without great coherence 'Learning Europe' Despite prevailing divergences in the economy and society, converging regulations and provision are being developed,	4. Balance and coherence: 'Towards a comprehensive European education and training system' The trend towards closer socio-economic cooperation is confirmed through pro-active

though the links to industry and private economy are largely missing. Efforts to ensure compatible rules and procedures at European level contribute little to increasing mobility and innovation. Systems and structures compete, and European matters are seen as peripheral.

cooperation between European Member States and pre-accession states in education and training. More people (young and old) are gaining higher levels of education and training. Resources are available through public and private funds.
Systems are developing in a comparable way. Qualification structures and educational/training provisions are becoming more and more similar and compatible.

The respondents were asked how likely they consider the overarching Cedefop scenarios to become reality. Below you can find the results.

QUESTION	NOT LIKELY	UNLIKELY	LIKELY/NOT LIKELY	LIKELY	VERY LIKELY
Divided Europe	11	5	7	4	0
Pick & mix Europe	2	11	8	4	2
Learning Europe	2	4	10	10	1
Towards a comprehensive European education and training system	1	3	9	8	6

As can be seen in the above table 'Divided Europe' isn't a likely scenario according to the respondents, nor is 'pick & mix Europe'. The other two scenarios are considered more likely, especially the 'Towards a comprehensive European education and training system' scenario.

We also asked the respondents their opinion on the importance of the scenarios. 'Divided Europe' is considered the least important, whereas 'Towards a comprehensive European education and training system' is the most important. The scenarios are on an ascending scale. The first scenario is regarded as not important, the second as a little bit more important, the third even more and the fourth is appreciated as the most important scenario.

QUESTION	NOT IMPORTANT		IMPORTANT/ NOT IMPORTANT		VERY IMPORTANT
Divided Europe	10	3	3	8	2
Pick & mix Europe	3	7	7	7	2
Learning Europe	2	4	6	9	5
Towards a comprehensive European education and training system	1	3	2	5	16

12. Annex V

12.1. List of country reports

Austria
Institut für Berufs- und Erwachsenen-Bildungsforschung (IBE) (2001). Scenarios and Strategies for VET in Europe. National Report Phase 2. Linz: Institute for Vocational & Adult Education Research at the Johannes Kepler University Linz (IBE).

Czech Republic
Kubátová, Helena et al (NITVE team) (2001). *Final National Report on Project Scenarios and Strategies of VET in Europe.* Praha: Research Institute of Technical and Vocational Education (VÚOŠ).

Estonia
Estonia Education Forum and Technical University (2001). *Scenarios and Strategies for Vocational Education and Training in Europe. Draft Final Report Estonia.* Tallinn: Estonia Education Forum and Technical University.

Germany
Philipp Grollmann, Wilfried Kruse, Felix Rauner (2001). Final German Report of the Cedefop/ETF Scenario Project. Final Report of the German Study of the Project Scenarios and Strategies for VET in Europe. Bremen: Institut für Technik & Bildung (ITB), Universität Bremen.

Greece
Dimoulas, K. & V. Papadogamvros. Scenarios and Strategies for VOcational Education and Training in Europe. The Greek case. Second National Report. Athens: Labour Institute GSEE - ADEDY.

Luxembourg/Belgium
Bedin, Jimmy (2001). Scenarios and Strategies for VET in Europe - Phase II. Report on Luxembourg and Belgium. Luxembourg: Etudes et Formation.

Poland
Kozek, Tadeusz & Rafal Piwowarski (2001). *Analysis of Scenarios and Strategies for VET in Poland.* Warsaw: BKKK - Cooperation Fund, Task Force for Training and Human Resources.

Slovenia
Faculty of Social Sciences, University of Ljubljana (2001). *Scenarios and strategies for VET in Europe. Country Report of Slovenia.* Ljubljana: Faculty of Social Sciences, University of Ljubljana.

United Kingdom
Leney, Tom & Mike Coles (2001). *Scenarios and strategies for training in the UK.* London: Institute of Education/Qualifications & Curriculum Authority.

13. Annex VI

13.1. References

Caldwell, Roger L. (1999) *University of Arizona on the World Wide Web:* http://www.ag.arizona.edu.

Doorn, J. van & F. van Vught (1981). *Nederland op zoek naar zijn toekomst.* Utrecht: Het Spectrum

European Training Foundation (1999). *On the World Wide Web:* http://www.etf.eu.int/etfwebnsf/pages/.

European Union (1999). *On the World Wide Web:* http://europa.eu.int/comm/cdp/scenario/resume/index_en.htm.

GBN (1999). Global Business Network on the World Wide Web: http://www.gbn.org.

Glenn, Jerome C. & Theodre J. Gordon (1997). *State of the Future; implications for action today. Millennium project.* Washington, D.C.: American Council for the United Nations University.

Godet, Michel. (1993). From anticipation to action: a handbook of strategic prospective. Paris: UNESCO Publishing.

Haselhoff, F. & E. Piëst (1992). Strategisch management. In J. Bilderbeek et al. (ed.). *Polybedrijfskundig Zakboekje.* Arnhem: PBNA.

Heijden, K. van der (1996). *Scenarios, The Art of Strategic Conversation.* Chichester: John Wiley & Sons Ltd.

Heijden, K. van der (1997). *Scenarios, strategies and the strategy process.* Nijenrode Research Paper Series, 1997-01. Breukelen: Nijenrode University Press.

Heus, P. de, R. van der Leeden & B. Gazendam (1995). Toegepaste Data-analyse; Technieken voor niet-experimenteel onderzoek in de sociale wetenschappen. Utrecht: Uitgeverij Lemma BV.

Jensen, Stefan et. al. (1972). Possible futures of European education, numerical and system's forecasts. In the series: Project I Educating man for the 21st century. The Hague: Martinus Nijhoff

Kahn, Herman & Anthony J. Wiener (1967). The year 2000 : a framework for speculation on the next thirty-three years. New York: Macmillan

Krijnen, H.G.(1993). De doelstellingen van de onderneming. In S. Douma (ed.). *Ondernemingsstrategie,* pp. 21 ff. Deventer: Kluwer.

Leeuw, A.C.J. de (1988). Organisaties: management, analyse, ontwerp en verandering. Assen: Van Gorcum.

McDaniel, O.C. (1998). Strategies for innovation in vocational education and training reform. ETF-AF98-007. Turin: ETF.

Mercer, David (1999). The Open University Business School on the World Wide Web: http://pcbs042.open.ac.uk.

Mintzberg, H. (1994). *The rise and fall of strategic planning.* Prentice Hall: Hemel Hempstead.

Mitroff, Ian I. (1983). *Stakeholders of the organisational mind.* San Francisco: Jossey-Bass.

OECD (1992). Technology in a Changing World. Paris: OECD.

OECD (1994). Science and Technology Policy: Review and Outlook. Paris: OECD.

OECD (1995). Learning Beyond Schooling: New Forms of Supply and New Demands. Paris: OECD.

OECD (1996). Education and Training: Learning and Working in a Society in Flux. Paris: OECD.

OECD (1999). Thematic Review of the Transition from Initial Education to Working Life. Paris: OECD.

OECD (1999). *Organisation for Economic Co-operation and Development on the World Wide Web:* http://www.oecd.org//els/edu/ceri/Objective/2/factsheet.htm#SCHOOLING FOR TOMORROW.

Ringland, Gill (1998). *Scenario planning; Managing for the Future.* Chichester: John Wiley & Sons Ltd.

Schoemaker, Paul J.H. (1991). When and How to Use Scenario Planning: A Heuristic Approach with Illustration. *Journal of Forecasting,* 10, pp. 549-564.

Schoemaker, Paul J.H. (1995). Scenario Planning: A Tool for Strategic Thinking. *Sloan Management Review,* Winter 1995, pp. 25-40.

Schwartz, Peter (1991). *Art of the Long View.* New York: Doubleday Currency.

Sellin, B., F. van Wieringen, H. Dekker, M. Tessaring & A. Fetsi (2001). *Scenarios and Strategies for Vocational Education and Training in Europe.* European synthesis report on phase I. MGK.01-50. Amsterdam: Max Goote Kenniscentrum bve.

Snuif, H.R. et al. (1991). *Het strategisch planningsproces in het midden- en kleinbedrijf in Noord-Nederland.* Den Haag: Vereniging voor strategische beleidsvorming.

The Millennium Project (1999). *Brief Overview on the World Wide Web:* http://www.geocities.com/~acunu/millennium/Millennium_Project.html

Wack, Pierre (1985a). Scenarios: uncharted waters ahead. *Harvard Business Review,* vol. 63 (5), p. 72.

Wack, Pierre (1985b). Scenarios: shooting the rapids. Harvard Business Review, vol. 63 (6), p. 139.

Wieringen, Fons van (1999). Scenario Planning for Vocational and Adult Education. *European Journal of Education,* vol 34, no 2, pp 153-175

Wieringen, A.M.L. van & V. Wessels (1998). Beroepsonderwijs in de toekomst. Scenario's en strategieën voor de BVE- en HBO-sector. Amsterdam: Max Goote Kenniscentrum bve.

Wieringen, Fons van & Graham Attwell (eds.).(1999). *Vocational and Adult Education in Europe.* Dordrecht: Kluwer Academic Publishers.

Wieringen, Fons van & Ghislaine Schmidt (June 2001). *Uncertanties in education: handle with care. Scenarios and strategies for VET in Europe.* First Outline for the Final Report. Draft. Amsterdam: Max Goote Kenniscentrum bve.

14. Selected Cedefop publications

Concerning the systems and developments of vocational education and training in Europe (for bibliographical details cf. www.cedefop.eu.int or www.trainingvillage.gr).

Regular reports: Vocational education and training in the European Member States

1996/1997
- Concepts and methodology for labour market forecasts by occupation and qualification in the context of a flexible labour market.
- Forecasting sectors, occupational activities and qualifications in the Federal Republic of Germany. A survey on research activities and recent findings.
- Key data on vocational training in the European Union.

1998
- Sectoral approach to training. Synthesis report on trends and issues in five European countries.
- Training for a changing society - A report on current vocational education and training research in Europe 1998 (2nd edition 1999). [First research report on VET in Europe].
- Vocational education and training - the European research field. Background report. 2 volumes [First research report on VET in Europe].
- Quality issues and trends in vocational education and training in Europe.
- Mobility and migration of labour in the European Union and their specific implications for young people.
- The impact on vocational training of studies. Analysing and forecasting trends in occupations. Case studies in Germany, The Netherlands and Denmark.
- New qualifications and training needs in environment-related sectors. Synthesis of studies carried out in Austria, Belgium, Denmark, Spain, France, Greece, Italy and the United Kingdom.
- Certificates, skills and job markets in Europe. A summary report of a comparative study conducted in: Germany, Spain, France, Italy, The Netherlands, United Kingdom.

- Recognition and transparency of vocational qualifications; The way forward. Discussion paper.

1999/2000
- European trends in the development of occupations and qualifications, 2 volumes.
- An age of learning: vocational training policy at European level (1st report on Vocational Training Policy in Europe).

Cedefop (European Centre for the Development of Vocational Training)

Future education: learning the future
Scenarios and strategies in Europe

Fons van Wieringen
Burkart Sellin
Ghislaine Schmidt

Luxembourg: Office for Official Publications of the European Communities

2003 – VI, 270 pp. – 17.6 x 25 cm

(Cedefop Reference series; 42 — ISSN 1608-7089)

ISBN 92-896-0200-7

Cat. No: TI-49-02-337-EN-C

Price (excluding VAT) in Luxembourg: EUR 25

No of publication: 3026 EN